NIGERIA'S CULTURAL TAPESTRY

Edited by

Moses Akinola Makinde

Occasional Publication
Number 12

Published by
The Nigerian Academy of Letters
Faculty of Arts, University of Ibadan
Ibadan, Nigeria

ISBN:1535327537

First Published in July, 2013

NAL Publications Committee

General Editor's Note

The theme of the Nigerian Academy of Letter's Annual Convocation in August 15 — 17, 2013 was *Nigeria's Cultural Tapestry*. The lead paper in this volume by Professor Ayodeji Olukoju is the key lecture delivered at that Convocation, at the University of Lagos, Akoka, Yaba, Lagos, on August 15, while the second lecture, under the same theme by Professor (Mrs.) Eno-Abasi Urua, was delivered at the same Convocation on August 15, 2013.

The third lecture by Professor Chidi T. Maduka was delivered at the Scientific Session of the Nigerian Academy of Letters' Annual Convocation, August 8— 10, 2012, at the University of Lagos, Akoka, Yaba, Lagos, under the theme, *The Literature of the ECOWAS Region.*

Notes on Contributors

— **Ayodeji Olukoju**, *FNAL*, is a Professor of History (Marine Economic History) and Vice-Chancellor, Caleb University, Imota, Lagos State.

— **Eno Abasi Urua** is a Professor of Linguistics and Nigerian Languages, University of Uyo, Uyo, Akwa Ibom State.

— **Chidi T. Maduka**, *FNAL*, is a retired Professor of Comparative Literature, University of Port Harcourt, Port Harcourt, Rivers State.

PREFACE: Presenting the Issues

1. Nigeria's Cultural Tapestry and the Challenge of Development

In his lecture, Prof Olukoju sees the theme of the Convocation as dwelling on the central issue of diversity which, according to him, he sees as critical to development in plural societies. He thinks it is a recurring issue in post-amalgamation history of Nigeria. In the main, the lecture reflects the author's "preoccupation with governance and development in changing historical contexts", by focusing on the "interlocking issues in leadership, governance, diversity and development". For him, a reference to tapestry evokes the image of "mosaic of cultures", outlining "how various ethnic groups work together in the US society". Surely, the author's reference to the US and the American reality of the "melting pot" model that has been used to describe the US will certainly be relevant to the Nigerian multicultural and plural societies.

On development and culture, the author gives four definitions of culture and argues that, although development too is open to many definitions, it is however better described than defined, citing the work of Said, Abdul Aziz on "Unity and Diversity" as a reference point. A critical issue in the lecture is the importance of the relationship between culture and development, with informed opinions suggesting that the two are interwoven, citing opinions from some authorities including, especially, the United Nations

Educational, Scientific and Cultural Organization (UNESCO) which States that "culture has been included in 70 per cent of the UN Development Assistance Frameworks".

The author illustrates with a Table 1, and Figure 1, on how culture contributes to developments. Under the figure, the author discusses the important issue 0h "Diversity" which he describes as a rubric covering disparities i:i cultural values, gender, ethnicity, age and religious beliefs, among others. For the author and especially for the Nigerian situation, what is of particular interest in his lecture is "ethnic diversity". Diversity is seen as necessarily conflict-ridden, a recipe for friction and disharmony. History is said to be replete with struggles by various nation-states to manage their problematic cultural or ethnic pluralism which, as he points out, has generally slowed down national development. But he notices a few exceptions, notably Penang, the most ethnically and racially diverse state of Malaysia where "ethnic and inter-ethnic connections rather than conflict, have created stability over a long period of time". As he further points out, although the negative effect of diversity in politics contrasts sharply with its utility in its positive force in business, the general consensus in political arena is that ethnic diversity is problematic and constitutes a slowdown in development. Quoting the economist Gustav Rains, the author points out that "ethnic diversity, especially in the sub-Saharan African context, is one of the causal factors behind relatively poor economic performance". He later gives several examples of the effect of established connection between ethnic diversity and economic underdevelopment, with relevant quotations from several authorities.

It is the opinion of the author that there is something to be gained from Nigerian cultural diversity, giving the example of the American cultural tapestry. Nigeria has failed to make use of its cultural diversity, unlike the US, because of "the traits in Nigerian daily life which constitute the source of its anti-developmental public culture that arises from the systematic and sustained subversion and bastardisation of the democratic system" in the first and subsequent republics, "the civil war and prolonged military rule, various ethno-regional eruptions and the mismanagement of the countries national resources, especially oil and gas". All of this, he, argues, has shaped our public culture, with systematic corruption as the chief defining feature of Nigeria's anti-developmental culture and greatest threat to the corporate existence of the country. Other cultures identified by the author include "settlement culture", "pathetic patronage", "corrupt patronage", "corruption and profligacy", "impunity" which he sees as the greatest common behavioural trait of players in the Nigerian space, "self-help" which is the weapon of the weak in the face of perceived injustice, the "docility" of Nigerians in the face of the suffocating grip of acquiescence to a decedent system and unwholesome practices by their rulers, leading to a pervasive culture of silence which is characterized by what Fela Anikulapo called "suffering and smiling" and, above all, living in denial, pretence and complicity with injustice and oppression. And he goes on to observe that although Nigerians can be aggressive when their national pride is wounded, most of them suffer from what he calls "culture cringe" inferiority complex that makes them see things foreign as superior or more attractive.

For the author, in spite of the positive things said about the experiences of more successful plural societies like US and Malaysia, our indigenous values contain elements that can enhance a new civic culture that can promote development. He then highlights those things we can revive in our culture in order to "remake" our nation, with examples drawn from the Igbo, Yoruba and Hausa-Fulani cultures, critically discussed. The rest of the lecture discusses what the author calls "The Qatari Challenge" and "Bridging the Diversity Development Divide: Lessons from Penang". According to the author, the transformation of Qatar from an oil-rich but underdeveloped wasteland into a regional aid global recognition in just 18 years is a big lesson for Nigerian leaders. Although Penang is the most ethnically diverse state in Malaysia, it has managed to harness that diversity to promote peaceful co-existence and social development (unlike Nigeria). He outlined some of the principles underlying the Penang experience based on a 21-point resolution as adopted at a Roundtable on cultural vibrancy in Penang.

As for Nigeria, he author writes on what he calls "the imperative of visionary leadership and the developmental state" to end his lecture. Some of these include his views that leadership in Nigeria needs a breakthrough, and must be bold, visionary, self-sacrificing and committed to leaving a worthy legacy. In his candid opinion, "the country can no longer afford to be led by megalomaniacs who are overwhelmed by the glamour of office, consumed by their self- importance, fixated on the next do or die elections while leaving undone urgent tasks of infrastructural development. Leadership and succession should not be left to chance, the Nigerian way. Nigeria needs an aristocracy talent in leadership positions, selected by achievement rather than by ascription".

In conclusion, the author reiterates his two central arguments: first, that diversity as such is not the cause of Nigeria's underdevelopment, and second, that ethno-linguistic fragmentation notwithstanding, there is a "supra-national development culture that drives bad governance and a poor sense of civic responsibility which has been the real threat to national development, unity and the people's well being". Finally, he admits that his lecture draws on elements in our indigenous history and culture, as well as other practices in other parts of the world, for him to suggest the possibilities of a counterculture which brings development that is humane and fair. For this reason, he submits that a better Nigeria is possible if, as he advocates, Nigerian history is taught in schools as a compulsory subject to equip young Nigerians with the sound knowledge of the history of the society they may have to govern in the future.

2.   Different Climes, Different Bird Songs: A Peep Into Nigeria's Linguistic Tapestry

In this lecture, Prof Eno-Abasi Urua discusses 'Nigeria's cultural tapestry' in the context of Nigeria's linguistic diversity. According to her, the linguistic diversity of Africa is not new. In fact, the claim has been made that, of the approximately 7000 languages worldwide, more than one third (over 2000) is found in Africa while over a quarter of that one third is found in Nigeria, with attention often drawn to the dense linguistic diversity in the West African region, particularly in the area between Nigeria and Cameroon. Nigeria itself is recorded as having over 500 languages. According to Brent Consulting, Nigeria is ranked 5th globally in language diversity.

In addressing Nigeria's linguistic tapestry, "tapestry" is discussed as diversities, which include the geographical, political, cultural and linguistic composition. The author zeroes in on the linguistic diversity, starting from the language families. Four language families are attested to in Africa viz., Niger Congo, Afro Asiatic, Nilo Saharan and Khoisan.

However, Nigeria is said to be home to three of the four, viz., Niger Congo, Nib Saharan and Afro Asiatic language families. She pointed out that about 75%of Nigeria's indigenous languages belong to the Niger Congo family, while Afro Asiatic is next with a mere 25%, and Nilo Saharan has just about two or three languages. Within Niger Congo, the Benue Congo sub group is said to have the largest number of languages in Nigeria. The implication, according to the author, is that most of Nigeria's "autochthonous languages" have a common heritage, suggesting "a concomitant common heritage for the people of Nigeria".

These languages have various fascinating characteristics spread across phonology (the sound system), morphology (word structure), syntax (sentence structure), sociolinguistics (language use in society) and orature (oral literature and folklore). Beyond showcasing these features, the lecture addresses the challenges of Nigeria as a linguistically diverse nation, taking a brief look at how other linguistically diverse countries such as South Africa and Sri Lanka have handled their diversity, and the lessons that we can learn therefrom. The lecture proffers suggestions on how we can harness our diversity for national integration and development.

In the "outlook and concluding" section, the paper suggests that, although there may be many autochthonous languages in Nigeria, these have a common ancestor in Niger Congo as seen in the various similarities found in the different languages. Although Nigeria seems to have an enormous number of autochthonous languages, which is part of its rich linguistic tapestry and cultural heritage, it is clear that many of these languages have a common lineage. The bulk of Nigeria's languages (about 75%) are from the Niger Congo language family showing the relatedness of these languages as is reflected in the similarities found in their basic vocabularies. In essence, there is therefore more that holds us together than the differences in these languages.

In order to avert the continued endangerment of the linguistic and cultural legacy and to ensure that these are preserved, the author calls on the Nigerian Academy of Letters (NAL) to establish and commission working groups for the investigation, compilation, classification, publication and preservation of the rich tapestry of various aspects of Nigeria's languages and cultures, including a Phonology group, a Morphology group, a Syntax group as well as an Oral Literature group.

3. The Artist as Griot: Two knives in the Widow's House

According to the dictionary definition, The Griot, in West Africa, especially in the past, is "a person who sings or tells stories about the history and traditions of their people and community". In this lecture, Prof. Maduka looks at the literature of the ECO WAS region, and closely examines the contribution of literature to the current struggle of the ECO WAS region's political leaders in ensuring not only the political and economic, but also the cultural unity of the ECOWAS countries. Looking at the studies of some scholars and their focuses on the region, the author argues that their individual treatment of materials focuses on their perception of the various authors as belonging to the same geographical area which, incidentally, were arbitrarily put together by their former colonial masters rather than sharing common political, economic and cultural affinities.

His interpretation of the theme of the Convocation — The Literature of the ECO WAS Region — leads him to what he considers the crucial questions, viz, "what is literature?" and "what is criticism?" In his opinion, the two questions are likely to provide stimulating responses to the theme of the Convocation.

About the griot, the author refers to many scholars in the ECO WAS region, like Okpewho, Blair, Finnegan,

13

Awonor, Azunonye, Sekoni and Senghor who have "reminded" us that the artist in the oral tradition is "basically a griot". The griot "is so multitalented that he could be a singer, a dancer, a poet, a novelist, a dramatist and a historian at the same time". Therefore one of the objectives of the author is to argue that contemporary writers in various languages like English, French, Hausa, Yoruba, Igbo, Tiv, Wolof, Akan, Ewe, and Idoma are all griots, or at least should be.

The author notices the relative importance accorded the various literatures in European and West African languages such as, for example, the West African languages: Hausa, Igbo, Yoruba, Tiv, Izon, Ibiobio, Kauru, Akan, Ewe, Bauce, Wolof e.t.c, but disagrees with the practice of favouring the literature in the so-called international languages, like English and French, over and above those of the West African languages.

The author further discusses what he calls the "Europeanization" of the literary scholarship in the ECO WAS region" as a result of the emigration of many of the seasoned African writers to Europe, and the development and use of theoretical frameworks and concepts borrowed from European practitioners, classicism, romanticism, realism, formalism, marxism, structuralism, sociology of Literature even with psychoanalytical approaches. Marxism is singled out by the author as one that has endeared itself to many West African scholars. He gives the names of some authors in this area and discusses their works in support of the Europeanization of literary scholarship in West Africa.

In another section, the author rehearses the arguments that characterize the struggle for the de-Europeanization of the criticism of African western writers "about a decade ago", a struggle that is more pronounced in the Anglophone section of the African literary experience. He also tries to sketch a possible theoretical position for interpreting West African texts in European and indigenous languages, especially in the work of Linda Tuhiwai Smith's classic, Decolonizing Methodologists: Research and Indigenous Peoples.

The author does not end his lecture without some advice. For him, attempts should be made to reorganize the programme of the West African languages departments in West African universities so that the students are taught how to read and write in a West African language, and also be able to interpret the literature in that language. In addition, a knowledge of oral literature should be made compulsory for both students and lecturers while comparative literature should be introduced in the appropriate departments as an integrated body of knowledge in order to promote unity among the various peoples of a country, the West African region and, indeed, the world. In conclusion, the author cautions West African scholars about using European critical theories in studying the literature of the ECOWAS region, as he thinks that the European theories are often formulated in, and with, ideas alien to the cultural experience of the region.

General Editor

Table of Contents

NIGERIA'S CULTURAL TAPESTRY AND THE CHALLENGE OF DEVELOPMENT

Professor Ayodeji Olukoju, FNAL

Preamble

President of the Nigerian Academy of Letters, permit me to begin by expressing gratitude to God and to the leaders of this Academy for giving me the privilege to deliver this lecture. When the College of Fellows, of which I am a member, chose the theme of this year's Convocation, I never imagined that I would be asked to deliver this lecture. This choice is a great honour that goes to my family, teachers, students, friends and the institutions that produced me. I will, therefore, approach this task with some measure of circumspection, if not trepidation, and a high sense of responsibility. However, do bear with me if I ruffle a few feathers in the course of this lecture.

Tapestry or Mosaic as Metaphor

President, Distinguished Ladies and Gentlemen, the theme of this year's Convocation, "Nigeria's Cultural Tapestry," dwells on the central issue of diversity, which is critical to development in plural societies. It is a recurring issue in the post-Amalgamation history of Nigeria. This is especially so in view of the challenges of nation- building which seem to have defied the best efforts of our leaders and countrymen. Hence, as a modest contribution to the discourse on diversity and development, I shall speak on **'Nigeria's Cultural Tapestry and the Challenge of Development.'** Please permit me to state some caveats from the outset. First, since I am not a literary or cultural studies expert, this presentation is not laden

17

with heavy postmodernist theory and arcane expressions. Second, as an eclectic historian, my presentation reflects my preoccupation with governance and development in changing historical contexts. Essentially, the lecture focuses on the interlocking issues of leadership, governance, diversity and development.

That said the lecture proceeds from the fundamental assumption that diversity is a fact of life, which has to be faced rather than erased. Hence, the reference to a "tapestry" evokes the image of a mosaic of cultures, each of which exercises its right to existence, alongside others. In a short essay on America's cultural tapestry, which outlined "How various ethnic groups work together in U.S. society," Gary Weaver (2008) explains that the metaphor of tapestry or mosaic better represents the current American reality than the "melting pot" model that had been used to describe the United States. The "melting pot" metaphor evokes images of the arrival of various peoples on American shores, each group contributing their peculiar cultures to an American pot in which the compound mass is heated till it melts into a new element, which is, however, dominated by the male White, Anglo-Saxon Protestant (WASP). The WASP "cookie- cutter" mould then fashions the various elements after its own image. But this development is more mythical than real in practice, especially with the passage of time and greater ethnic diversity. Hence, unchangeable cultural and physical features defied the mould, retaining the American diversity as we now know it. Weaver, therefore, presents tapestry/mosaic as a better representation of the American cultural reality. For, in a mosaic or tapestry, each colour retains its identity but adds to the overall beauty of the object. To remove a piece from a mosaic or a thread from the tapestry, he asserts, is to destroy it. Consequently, diversity is a positive force and tampering with it through homogenization would damage its essence and utility. This raises the bigger issue of the relationship between diversity and development, the core of this lecture. But first, a discussion of the connection between culture and development.

Culture and Development

"Culture" and "Development" are two of the most difficult concepts to define as there are probably as many definitions as the number of writers on the subjects. It has been suggested, for example, that there are "at least four contested definitions of culture." (Nurse, 2006:35). These are:

- a developed state of mind (when we say, for example, "s/he is a cultured person")
- the processes of this development (with reference to "cultural interests" or "cultural activities"; or, Wallerstein's distinction between "production cultures" and "consumption cultures" Nurse, 2006: 38)
- the means of these processes ("the arts" or "humane intellectual works")
- "a whole way of life" or "a signifying system" which provides a lens through which society or a social order is reproduced, experienced, communicated or explored (Nurse, 2006: 35, citing Williams, 1981: 11-13)

"Development," too, is open to diverse definitions, and it is better described than defined. According to Said (2004:9):

development is a historical process through which human beings choose and create their future within the context of their environment to achieve a humanist and creative society. It is concerned with the dignity of the individual - that level of self-esteem and self-awareness that is secure and self-accepting and the restructuring of the institutions and culture of society to support such ends.

Generally, development encompasses the physical, material and spiritual changes in society which produced consistent improvements in the wellbeing of the people. But while the steady and consistent growth of the economy, improvements in lifestyle, educational standards and technology are quantifiable and measurable, intangible things such as emotional wellbeing, cannot be quantified. Hence, development is relative, contextual and nonlinear.

What is of immediate importance is the relationship between the two. Informed opinion holds that culture and development are interwoven. According to the United Nations Educational, Scientific and Cultural Organisation (UNESCO):

> *Development interventions that are responsive to the cultural context and the peculiarities of a place and community, and advance a human-centred approach to development are most effective, and likely to yield sustainable, inclusive and equitable outcomes.* (UNESCO, 2012:5)

Hence, since January 2O1 2, culture has been included in 70 per cent of the UN

Development   Assistance   Frameworks.
(UNESCO, 2012: 3, note 2).

In general, culture may be said to be key to development in the following areas. First, as a contributor to the global economy, tourism is one of the fastest growing business sectors. Cultural tourism accounts for 40 per cent of total world tourism revenues. Second, investment in culture-related activities has revitalised the economies of major cities, which utilize cultural heritage and cultural events to improve their image, attract investment and visitors and stimulate urban development. Third, culture-led development has also facilitated greater social inclusiveness and rootedness, innovation, creativity and small-scale business enterprises. Fourth, culture has also been critical to sustainable development. Indeed, it has been described as the fourth pillar of sustainable development. (Nurse, 2006) Fifth, sound knowledge and application of local culture has built trust between development agencies and local end users, and ensured a proper insertion of new technologies and ideas into local contexts. Sixth, culture aids development by the acknowledgement of the virtues of cultural diversity and respect for individual human rights, and the promotion of sustainable environmental management practices.

[1] UNESCO, 2012:4, for the discussion in this paragraph.

Finally, inter-cultural dialogue has also prevented or/and mitigated conflicts, and protected the rights of marginal and minority groups. (Akinyele, 2013)

In proposing an optimal synergy between culture and development, UNESCO (2010) produced a Culture for Development Indicator Suite, which demonstrates how seven policy areas or "Dimensions" (Economy, Education, Heritage, Communication, Governance and Sustainability; Social; Participation; and Gender Equality) and their sub-dimensions function in a framework of culture for development. (See Table 1)

Table 1: Dimensions and Sub-Dimensions of Culture for Development

Dimensions	Sub-dimensions
Economy	1. Added value of cultural activities to GDP 2. Employment in culture 3. Household expenditures on culture
Education	1. Complete, fair and inclusive education for all 2. Valorization of interculturality, cultural diversity and creativity in the first two years of secondary school 3. Training of professionals in the cultural sector
Heritage	1. Promotion and valorization of heritage
Communication	1. Freedom of Expression 2. Access and Internet use 3. Diversity of media content
Governance and Institutionality	1. Standard-setting framework for culture 2. Policy and institutional framework for culture 3. Distribution of cultural infrastructure 4. Civil society participation in cultural governance

Social Participation	1. Participation in cultural activities
	2. Trust
	3. Freedom of self- determination
Gender Equality	1. Levels of gender equality
	2. Perception of gender equality

Source: UNESCO, 2010: Accessed at:
http://www.unesco.org/new/en/culture/themes/culturaldiv
ersity/diversity-ofcultural-
expressions/programmes/culture-for-development
indicators/seven-dimensions/, 9 June 2013.

UNESCO (2012: 7-8) has also proposed the following practical recommendations toward dovetailing culture with development:

1. That culture should be integrated into governance, in the conception, measurement and practice of development, to make development inclusive, equitable and sustainable.
2. That sustainable cultural tourism, cultural and creative industries, cultural institutions and culture-based urban revitalisation be promoted as catalysts of local entrepreneurship, employment generation and local development.
3. That fragile cultural assets be protected as a unique and nonrenewable cultural capital.
4. That traditional knowledge and practices should be integrated into sustainable environmental schemes to foster environmental sustainability.
5. That culture be deployed in promoting social cohesion through intercultural dialogue while the arts could be

harnessed to develop local entrepreneurship among the youth in post-conflict and post-disaster situations.

Figure 1 illustrates the UNESCO proposal for synergizing culture and development.

Fig. 1: **How Culture Contributes to Development**

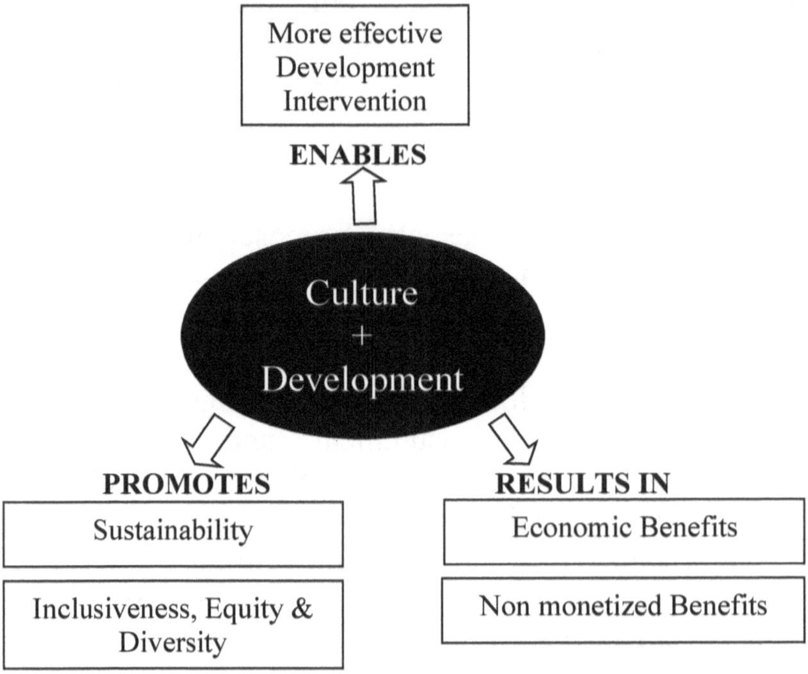

Source: UNESCO, 2012: 8.

Culture and Development: Diversity as Recipe for Disaster?

'Diversity" as a rubric covers disparities in cultural values, gender, ethnicity, age and religious beliefs, among others. What is of interest in this lecture is ethnic diversity, for which "diversity'1 serves as an alternate. A dominant narrative in scholarly and popular discourse is that diversity is necessarily conflict-ridden, that it is in/of itself a recipe for friction and disharmony. History is replete with struggles by various nation-states to manage their problematic cultural or ethnic pluralism, which has generally hobbled national development. A notable exception has been Penang (discussed later in this lecture), the most ethnically (that is, racially) diverse State in Malaysia, where "ethnic solidarities   and inter-ethnic connections rather than conflict, have created stability over long periods of time." (Evers, 2012) "High and increasing diversity," with the arrival of more immigrants to Penang, it has been noted, "poses a challenge for good governance, but also provides the basis for the upcoming innovative knowledge-based economy and society." (Evers, 2012)

The negative valuation of diversity in politics contrasts sharply with its utility in management theory, which makes it a positive force in business. Hence, "diversity management" serves a positive role as an attribute in business. Big organizations deliberately create diverse teams to harness the potential of their pool of multinational or multi-racial operatives for innovation and creativity. Such practices have generally engendered competitiveness and improved performance. (Evers, 2012)

Returning to the political scene, the general consensus is that ethnic diversity is problematic and constitutes a drag on development. "There seems to be a general consensus, based on both cross- country regressions and individual country studies," notes the leading economist Gustav Ranis, "that ethnic diversity, especially in the Sub-Saharan

African context, is one of the causal factors behind relatively poor economic performance." (Ranis, 2011:3)

This is buttressed by numerous studies on the connection between diversity on the one hand, and conflict and economic crises on the other.(Goren, 2013) However, there is a debate over which of ethnic polarisation or ethnolinguistic fractionalisation (ELF) inflicts greater damage on economic development. In a well-cited article (Collier and Gunning, 1999), it was claimed that ELF alone accounts for 35% of growth deficit in Sub-Saharan Africa (SSA) and for 45% when taken together with some policy issues. However, Montalvo and Renal-Querol (2005), in ancther well-cited article, also established the connection between ethnic diversity and economic underdevelopment but attri1uted this to ethnic polarisation instead of ELF Their argument was that: " Where there are social cleavages, there are frictions among social groups. When the society is divided by religious, ethnolinguistic, or race differences, tensions emerge along these divisions. (Montalvo and Renal-Querol, 2005: 308) They pointed out that resources that should have been invested in generating economic growth were diverted into nonproductive inter-group competition. Where tension between competing groups bred instability and uncertainty, these would reduce investment. Their extensive statistically-backed analysis led them to the conclusion that: "an increase in social polarization has a negative effect on growth because it reduces the rate of investment and increases public consumption and the incidence of civil wars." (Montalvo and Renal-Querol, 2005: 318) Other authors, such as Easterly and Levine (1997), also contend that ethnolinguistic polarisation delays or prevents quick resolutions leading to positive public policies and that it promotes rent-seeking activities, undermines trust, raises transaction costs and has an adverse effect on development. (Ranis, 2011)

In terms of nation-building and governance, a popular solution to diversity (where ethnic groups live together in a defined geographical space, such as a nation-state) has been the adoption of the federal system of government, which has many variants. However, federalism or unity in diversity, has never been universally popular. Indeed, it has been debunked as aggravating, rather than ameliorating, the knotty situation. There is the school of thought that parlays the myth of Africa's pre-colonial cultural unity and peaceful co-existence, and advances a narrative that it was colonialism that made diversity a veritable avenue to political instability, so pronounced in most post-independence African countries. Colonialism or, more generally, imperialism has been fingered as the critical culprit in the underdevelopment of Africa, exploiting the fault-lines of ethnic diversity. In my undergraduate years at the University of Nigeria, Nsukka, the popular speakers of the day -Professor Ikenna Nzimiro and Drs. Inyang Eteng and Chuba Okadigbo, never ceased to invoke the title of a much lampooned article, 'The Inevitability of Instability" (O'Connell, 1967), to loud guffaws to advance the argument that if diversity was a problem at all, it was the imperialists that had manipulated it to sow discord. In the same context, Chief Obafemi Awolowo's reference to Nigeria as a "mere geographical expression" drew much flak and his advocacy of federalism was presented as compounding rather than solving the problem.

This lecture seeks to engage this narrative and explore the possibility of a counter-narrative that dwells more on how to trascend diversity by harnessing it to achieve societal development. It acknowledges the undeniable debilitating contributions of the slave trade, colonialism, the digital divide, globalization and differential human and natural resource distribution to the underdevelopment of African countries. But it projects the absence of good governance anchored on the developmental state and focused leadership as the missing link between diversity and development.

The Nigerian Cultural Tapestry: The Poverty of Civic/Public Culture

Returning to our earlier reference to the American cultural tapestry, it is necessary to clarify an important point the mosaic combines diversity with a dominant, defining national culture. In the American case, the dominant national culture encompasses the predominant values shared by a vast majority of the people and which drives official policies, as well as corporate and individual action. According to Weaver, regardless of their diversity, Americans hold certain values or aspirations dear, such as emphasis on individual achievement, class mobility and distrust of an overly powerful central government, a common language (though Spanish is a second official language in many States) and standing united behind the Stars and Tripes the national flag. The emphasis on personal achievement, which fuels social mobility, is illustrated by the habit of the average

American introducing him/herself by what s/he does for a living rather than by his/her family background or origins. Hence, according to Weaver, it is usual for an average American to tell a stranger his name and profession - that is what they do - while for a Nigerian, for example, the likely emphasis would be on his state of origin, lineage or some other reference to who s/he is.

There are, of course, exceptions to this generalization. It only goes to show what premium each society places on indices of identification and recognition. Americans also share a rejection of the monarchical form of government, given the experience of the first immigrants from Europe, and the glorification of rugged individualism that accords more with republicanism. This extends to a suspicion of "big government," captured by Henry David Thoreau's maxim: "less government is better government." Again, there are exceptions to this general rule in times of national crises, such as wars and economic depression. I am not painting a utopian picture of America, which has its own Archiles heels in gun violence, youth deliquency and institutionalised racism, just as other nations grapple with their own challenges.

What can be deduced from the experiences of the United States and many other countries is that it is that public/civic culture, the aggregate of the shared values of the people(s), as articulated in daily life and subscribed to by their leaders and ordinary people, that shapes the fortunes of the nation itself. Consequently, national character that flows from such shared values largely determines the social, political and economic fortunes of the people.

Many people steeped in the idea of a Nigerian diversity characterized by ethnic-based cultures assume that there is no dominant pan-Nigerian culture, to which a large number of Nigerians subscribe and which defines our national character within and outside the country. This erroneous impression is corrected in the discussion in this section. The aim is to demonstrate that it is informal culture in the public sphere that accounts for what Nigeria is today, the same way American public culture has driven the United States to where it is today.

The post-independence history of Nigeria has been dominated by certain key events, including the systematic and sustained subversion and bastardisation of the democratic system in each of the First and subsequent republics; civil war and prolonged military rule; various ethno-regional eruptions; and the mismanagement of the country's natural resources, especially, crude oil and natural gas. These events shaped what I have termed the country's national public culture, which has largely determined the fortunes of the country. My position is that it is those elements of our public culture, much more than any foreign imperialist or neo-imperialist agenda, that account for the Nigerian situation. These traits in Nigerian daily life constitute the sinews of Nigeria's anti-developmental public culture.

Constituents of Nigeria's Anti-Developmental Public Culture

Regardless of protestations to the contrary, public culture in Nigeria is dominated by most, if not all, of these features. Due allowance may be made for the contexts in which Nigerians live or operate. An attempt will be made to give historical depth to these features by citing examples from Nigeria's post-independence history.

It is an understatement to declare rapine or systemic corruption to be the chief defining feature of Nigeria's anti-developmental culture and the greatest threat to the corporate existence of the country. The scale or quantum has grown exponentially since independence. In the First Republic, the scale of corruption was apparently limited by the quantum of resources available for plunder, and by the   relatively more developed   public   spiritedness   of   the leading   political   leaders   of   the   era. Nevertheless, it was   not unknown. Even the corrupt governors and ministers of the Gowon era (1966-75) appear   saintly   compared   to   their   more   rapacious successors. So rife and systemic has corruption become that things have become worse with each passing regime since the Second

Republic of Shehu Shagari, which eventually collapsed under the weight of profligacy, corruption and electoral malfeasance. The cancer of corruption and political sleight of hand became systemic and symptomatic of the Babangida regime, which was largely associated with the "settlement" culture. Abacha's brutal regime superintended the looting of the till leading to the flight of billions of dollars into overseas bank accounts, much of which is still being traced.

The "settlement culture" manifests in two ways. The first one is: "don't ruffle feathers, just suck it up, let's cover the shame, let's forgive and forget, and let's pretend the evil never happened so as not to expose our friend or our man/brother." We enjoy sweeping dastardly acts under the carpet in the name of settlement. The other type of settlement culture is that there is no case that has no price. Hence, you hear people talk of "name your price" and this has gradually become a way of life for Nigerians.

Yet another is the culture of pathetic patronage. Family and associates pester persons who have just been elected into office for corrupt patronage. Undue pressure is mounted on public office holders to pay back financiers (so-called political godfathers) after elections. Contracts are awarded after every election to people who lack the technical competence, managerial experience or resources to handle the projects. Abandoned contracts are never probed, and released funds are never recovered because of our culture of "not opening old wounds," best described by the story of three proverbial monkeys: "see no evil, hear no evil, speak no evil." Consequently, public money now grows wings in billion-naira scams. No nation has ever developed under the albatross of the purloining of the public purse.

A corollary of systemic and endemic corruption is profligacy, the mindless waste of public resources. This, too, has become a great drag on Nigeria's developmental efforts. Granted that Nigeria earns a fairly steady income from crude oil and natural gas exports (with all the perils of a monocultural economy), the country is still relatively poor. Its poverty is revealed by the huge deficits in infrastructure, education, healthcare and local content in industry and critical sectors of the economy, which the totality of internally generated revenue, even with prudent management, cannot possibly fund. Yet, Nigerian leaders have rather focused on white elephant - the proverbial bridge to nowhere: the under-utilized seaports and airports, prestige projects without economic spin-offs - which would yield slush funds to oil the corrupt politicians' campaign and election and saddle the people with sub-standard infrastructure, which benefits only a small fraction of the population. Driven by megalomania and a bloated sense of Nigeria's importance, Nigeran officials take very large and bloated delegations to regional, continental and global summits. A retinue of officials accompanies our athletes and sports ambassadors to international engagements. Presidents and governors undertake countless and useless overseas trips, especially the quizotic search for foreign investors, with a huge entourage, all drawing estacode from our national patrimony. The rate at which public officials and their friends acquire a fleet of aircraft and put the latest models of exotic cars on pothole-infested roads betrays the absence of a developmental vision and a lack of self-confidence in our so-called leaders.

It may be argued that next to corruption and profligacy, the greatest common behavioural trait of players in the Nigerian public space is impunit3 and this is not a recent development. As early as the First Republic, notable people and/or their agents committed offences against the State and its citizens, and were not made to face the full wrath of the law. In consequence, such misdemeanour was repeated in later times. For example, the mayhem in the Western House of Assembly in May 1962 was perpetrated by some so-called "Honourables," who broke the mace, assaulted their colleagues and disrupted proceedings. Till date none was brought to book. The recent affray on the floor of the Rivers State House of Assembly merely rehashed that script. Elections were brazenly rigged in the Western Region in 1964-65, and again in August 1983. In spite of court decisions and/or graphic evidence, the culprits got away with it. In the case of the perennial cancellation of elections in Oguta, Imo State, a commentator, who identified federal lawmakers from the area as major culprits stated as follows: 'Any inquisition that ignores the brazen impunity displayed by these elected federal legislators will be patently meaningless." He added that it had become "paramount to check the impunity of these ... people." (Omeihe, 2013)

Another trait that dominates public behaviour is self-help, which is widely acknowledged as the weapon of the weak in the face of perceived injustice. Violent reactions to electoral heist, perceived to have been perpetrated by unpopular but powerful state actors with the connivance of judicial and security apparatus of State, have characterized most elections in post-independence Nigeria. Western Nigeria achieved notoriety for the "wet e" spree of arson, destruction of property and murder of political opponents in 1964-65 and in Ondo State in 1983. Sporadic violence also greeted disputed elections in parts of the West, Benue and Akwa Ibom States in more recent times. Self-help can be regarded as an indignant response to weak institutions, brazen injustice and impunity, and the "might-is-right" syndrome. The "might-is-right" type of self-help, typical of powerful Nigerians who abduct creditors or demolish physical structures or forcibly possess disputed land, was recently demonstrated in a long-drawn dispute between two agencies of the federal government. On June 21, 2013, the Nigerian Maritime Administration and Security Agency (NIMASA)

[2] The author's father, Hon. Israel Adeniyi Olukoju, escaped the mayhem and remained with the Action Group.

blockaded the Bonny Channel to compel the Nigeria Liquified and Natural Gas (NLNG) company to pay a disputed levy. The blockade defied a High Court injunction in favour of the gas company. A newspaper (*The Nation*, 8 July 2013:19) declared that it was "hard to find a more befitting word than self-help" to describe the NIMASA action. Given the intervention of the court, the paper wondered why NIMASA was "in a hurry to do things its own way." But this was merely one in a long list of cases of self-help, mainly among private persons, between government agencies and private concerns, and, as in this case, between government establishments. No nation can develop in such an atmosphere of lawlessness.

What is also becoming alarmingly rife in the Nigerian public space is the suffocating grip of acquiescence to a decadent system and unwholesome practices by the populace. It is reflected in the robotic obedience to unlawful orders by police orderlies who brutalize fellow citizens on the orders of their power-drunk principals. For instance, the brutal treatment of a journalist, Minere

Amakiri, by the military governor of Rivers State, Alfred Diete-Spiff, in 1973 was done by underlings in obedience to what was a patently inhumane order. A commentator asserted that: "Nigerians are specially gifted at rising or falling to the level of leadership they're offered."(Ogunlesi, 2013:25)

There is a pervasive cult of silence in Nigeria. It is called "suffering and smiling," living in denial, pretence, and complicity with injustice and oppression. It manifests in a herd instinct (Fela's "follow-follow") or the "if you cannot beat them, join them" syndrome. For instance, those who should have spoken out kept quiet till the Boko Haram insurgency in the North invaded even the hallowed chambers of emirs' palaces. The bandwagon mentality and appeasement of the "winner-by foul means" or worship of the parvenu ("money-miss-road") betrays moral cowardice. Sycophancy, eye service, obsequiousness and hero-worship are routinely expressed in fawning congratulatory messages to temporary holders of power on occasions of inconsequential "achievements" or "landmarks." Even an octogenarian could address a lady half his age but fortunate to be a First Lady, as 'our mother," even when Her Excellency's conduct belies the title.

Where nepotism ("man-know-man") reigns, mediocrity becomes the norm. Banality takes centre stage and reaches new depths in the craving for titles, especially Honorary Doctorates. Even institutions that do not award bachelor's degrees brazenly award all manner of doctorate degrees, often styled "fellowships," and those institutions that do not have the professoriate now organize inaugural lectures! It seems that we have chosen to settle for second-best and sub-standard products, leaders, facilities and what have you.

Sheer mendacity brazen lying as an art of governance - what the inimitable Professor Emeritus Tekena Tamuno has styled "lying-state" has become official policy. Endorsement now supersedes voting and sixteen votes are higher than nineteen! Official double- speak makes it difficult to know what and who to believe. Usually reliable sources are now suspect. The credibility of government as an institution is eroded and public trust in the integrity of our leaders is weakened.

In a materialistic world, hedonism and excess should be expected. But the degree and pervasiveness of godless, soul-less greed ("chop and quench"; *jeun ko'ku"*), avaricious and vulgar materialism, loud and raucous exhibitionism, vanity ("I better pass my neighbour"), get-rich-quick mentality beat the imagination. Our materialism is tasteless and gaudy. We love grandeur and pomp without quality and substance. We are notorious, even in Europe and North America, for our ostentatious celebrations of empty "landmarks." A columnist lamented that: "Those who should be laying out the framework for reconditioning our minds are too busy overcelebrating underachievements, too busy building castles on the ground for themselves and in the air for the people." (Ogunlesi, 2013:25)

Although Nigerians can be aggressive when their national pride is wounded, most suffer from "culture cringe1' inferiority complex that makes all things foreign superior or more attractive. Anything foreign seems fine, if not better than ours. Foreign degrees, foreign accent, foreign spouses and elaborate wedding ceremonies in foreign lands (Dubai, the UK, the USA, etc.) have now become status symbols.

Nigeria has produced many authors and easily dominates any list of winners of competitive scholarly fellowships and the like in Africa. Yet, obscurantism appears to have been adopted as an official policy. We seem to have canonised illiteracy. The 'no-nothing' syndrome has given meaning to the popular saying: "I no know book o." Once you have money, it seems, that covers a multitude of your inadequacies.

In politics, when driving on the highway and everywhere else, we resort to brinkmanship and muscle-flexing. Nigerian public culture is replete with one-upmanship and grandstanding. People of power, who should have known better, huff and puff over petty issues of ego and neglect the fundamental issues that concern the vast majority of their subjects. We do not need an accountant to tell us that huge sums of money have gone down the drain as the ongoing ridiculous power show in Rivers States the shame of the Black race enters another round. And the common people are the worse for it. In all of this, Nigerians have murdered public shame, opprobrium and outrage. Nothing shocks us any more.

It is commonly acknowledged that the lack of strong institutions is a major hindrance to development in these parts. It is one thing for the institutions to be fledgling and in need of nurturing. But it is a different matter if Nigerians engage in a favourite pastime: institution-wrecking. It is done with relish as long as it serves a narrow interest,such as unleashing security and anti-corruption agencies against your political rivals, or suborning the electoral commission and the judiciary to facilitate vote-rigging. In one stroke, you effortlessly destroy EFCC, INEC and the judiciary.

One would have thought that in a system that has been run for over fifty years Nigerians would have mastered the art of planning. Sadly, where strategic plans and budgets exist at all, they are treated as monuments or documents to be shelved, or glazed and displayed. Hence, we always resort to last-minute measures, ad-hocism, fire brigade approach in an atmosphere of uncertainty and unpredictability. This is why we perform poorly at major global sporting events because we always leave everything till too late or to chance. Yet, when we want to move at all, at the eleventh hour, we now scramble and stampede to beat the deadline. Much energy is wasted and such haste is often without progress and this amounts to effort without efficiency.

After we have failed to plan and actually planned for failure, we begin to search for scapegoats, usually political opponents and other adversaries, real or imagined. Ultimately, we resort to fatalism in the garb of religiousity. We explain away our failures to the will of God or the designs of Satan, as the case may be.

The way we handle our waste says much about our national character. Whereas the Japanese, for example, have simplified things through a disciplined use of sorting-at-source, we have mastered the shot-put and "not-in-my-backyard" method of litter proliferation and waste dumping. To physical waste, we have added noise pollution.

Unlike the colonial period, where there was noise control in Lagos, Nigerian cities (and increasingly, too, the suburban and rural areas) are notorious for the cacophony of uncontrolled noise from honking vehicles, brawlers, hawkers, entertainers and preachers. Even university campuses are no longer immune.

What runs through our public conduct is incivility, even in high places. Beyond the 'uncivil society' of motor park touts and the like, the hallowed chambers of legislative houses have often been turned into boxing rings without referees and rules of engagement, as exhibited in Rivers State a few weeks ago.

But this was not always the case and should not continue to be. We need to develop a template for good governance, anchored on our cultural values to promote development.

An Indigenous "Good Governance" Template?: Towards an Enduring, Developmental Civic Public Culture

The parlous state of our public culture belies the existence of developmental cultural traits in our indigenous societies. Without prejudice to what we have outlined from the experiences of more successful plural societies, our indigenous values contain elements that can enhance a new civic culture that promotes development. Drawing on the record of Nigerian history and the rich repertoire of our traditions, this section highlights what we can revive in our civic culture to remake our nation.

It is often assumed that Nigerian peoples have never had traditions of good governance even in their village settings. Such misconception could have been informed by the fact that they did not have formal, written constitutions, with elaborate sections and provisions as most nations have today. But, as is well known, there are nations today that do not have a formal constitution or have a threadbare one. The point is that Nigerian peoples practised in their different settings versions of good governance that suited their peculiar epochs. (cf. Ajayi and Ikara, 1985; Osuntokun and Olukoju, 1997)

While the Igbo of Eastern Nigeria did not have a formal constitution, each village had a conception of "development" as its members understood it, and the vast majority of the people imbibed norms of participation, majoritarianism and consensus-building. The same can be said for other non-monarchical or republican groups, though we must admit that Lugardian indirect rule and the quest for a so-called fulcrum of authority pushed many communities to adopt some form of monarchical rule. This has since been exacerbated among the Igbo, where the kingship institution has spread beyond the western flank stretching from Onitsha to Oguta. But the point is that ideals of participation ("one person, one vote"), freedom of expression and consensus building can still be promoted as a cultural virtue in modern Nigeria, where it often seems that might is right and a minority can brazenly claim victory in elections.

As for the Yoruba, they operated a constitutional monarchical system that effectively checked the autocracy of a single person, who sometimes was made to pay the ultimate price for breaching the unwritten constitution. For example, an unwanted Alaafin was presented with an empty calabash or a parrot's egg as a sign that he had outlived his usefuleness and must step aside by committing suicide. Not only was succession not by primogeniture, it also rotated among various branches of the ruling house. This entailed some form of selection, if not election in some cases. Of course, this was an oligarchy, from which women were mostly excluded, but it was not an absolute monarchy or the autocratic democracy that many so-called modern nations practise today. From the Yoruba worldview, we can deduce the virtues of checks on arbitrary power and the focus on government as a means to an end - "development." Hence the goal of *"itesiwaju"* (literally, "progress") or *"olaju"* ("civilisation") can be attained through politics ("oselu", which literally means "developing the community/polity") as opposed to what Chief Obafemi Awolowo called *"ojelu"* (plunder/rapine - literally, "eating up the community/polity"), when referring to corrupt politicians.

If it appears that the Islamic polities of northern Nigeria had been monarchical right from the pre-jihad era, we should not lose sight of the codifications of norms that governed public civic culture. A striking illustration of this the fact that governance was taken seriously and guided by some publicly declared rules is that at least two treatises were written and circulated in the Central Sudan. During the reign of *Sarkin Kano* Muhammad Rumfa (d.1499), the celebrated Muslim cleric Muhammad b. Abd al-Karim al-Maghili al-Tiemsani (better known as Al-Maghili) authored a treatise, *Risalat al-Muluk* (*The Obligations of Princes*), which spelt out Islamic standards of good governance for the guidance of Rumfa, who was a notable Muslim in his own right. Two other examples from the early nineteenth-century history of the Sokoto Caliphate further illustrate the historical depth of the idea of a governance template.

First, the leader of the Sokoto jihad, Uthman dan Fodio, authored the Kitab al-Farq (A Book of Distinction), in which he distinguished the practices of non-Islamic polities from those of the envisaged Islamic State. It is interesting that when the ulama al-sui, who were embedded in the power structure or siyasa (politics) of the day criticised him for preaching without separating women from the men, he countered that it was a minor and forgivable infraction compared to the greater fitna of keeping women in ignorance. From this we could see that Dan Fodio himself had struck an early blow in favour of girl-child or women education even in a conservative Islamic setting. Small wonder that the cleric's own daughter, Nana Asma'u, was a poetess and celebrated author in her own right. Not only did Dan Fodio promote women literacy, he practised what he preached in his own household, unlike most modern leaders today. Second, in c.1807, in the early years of the ihad, Uthman dan Fodios brother, Abdullahi, a poet and lawyer, was so disgusted with the manifestation of worldliness among the jihaddists that he abandoned the struggle for a pilgrimage to the East. However, on getting to Kano, the local reformists prevailed on him to abandon his eastward journey. During his sojourn in Kano, where he also observed some deviations, he composed at his hosts' request a treatise on how to run the government according to the tenets of

I owe the insights in the discussion that follows to my Final Year Special Paper on The Sokoto Caliphate, taught by Professor C. N. Ubah, at the University of Nigeria, Nsukka. But I take responsibility for selection of source material and interpretations.

Islam. Abdullahi dan Fodio's *Diya' al-Hukkam (The Light of the Rulers or The Principles of Government)* was a sort of governance template for the emergent Kano emirate. It is a moot point whether any ruler in that part of the country is guided by that document or any other on good governance.

Other examples can be cited from local settings across Nigeria. What is worth stressing is that our traditional values and practices should be re-visited to harness those that can help us to re-invent the culture of civility and developmental governance. How a society treats its women and what it does about peaceful co-existence or the treatment of so-called strangers tell much about its level of development. This is true of Nigerian communities even in precolonial times.

The role of women in various societies is a case in point. In practically all Nigerian societies, even in the matrilineal ones, women have played second fiddle to men, even their own sons and younger brothers. Yet, women have also exercised soft power, which often affected the directions of state policy. The point is that many Nigerian communities recognise and accord women certain roles that men did not play. For example, till date, women are preferred as regents in some kingdoms; in some others they held titles and took part in direct decision making in the highest councils, though always as a minority. In practically all societies, women entrepreneurship was the norm, even when cultural practices limited their mobility. Where they suffered no such restrictions, they accumulated wealth, owned property and played overt politics. The mythical Queen Amina, the historical Madame Tinubu of Lagos and Abeokuta, Efunsetan Aniwura of Ibadan and Omu Okwei of Ossomari, or the more modern examples Alimotu Pelewura of Lagos, Funmilayo Ransorne-Kuti of Abeokuta, Margaret Ekpo of Calabar, Gambo Sawaba, the stormy petrel of Northern Nigeria, Humaini Alaga of Ibadan and Abibatu Mogaji of Lagos literally rocked the cradle and the crown, often tempestously.

The treatment of settlers, now a bone of contention in modern Nigeria, is a key issue in the evolution of a developmental public culture. Plateau State has been a theatre of war and various Nigerian communities (Umuleri/Aguleri; Onitsha/Obosi; Warn (Urhobo and Izon versus Itsekiri) and Ile-Ife/Modakeke) have at various times demonstrated our abandonment of the cardinal principle of good neighbourliness and concern for strangers, so-called. It is instructive in this regard, and this is documented by Adamu Fika (1978: 158, n.82), that Yoruba-speaking peoples had settled in Iyagi and Yakasai quarters of Kano since the seventeenth century. There was no report that they were molested, massacred or expelled at any time during the pre-colonial era. Hausa and Nupe communities have been in Yorubaland for centuries, intermarrying with host communities. In spite of the conflict that accompanied the rise of the Sokoto Caliphate, trade continued across the ecological divide between northern and southern Nigeria. While not painting an unrealistic picture of unbroken harmony, this writer suggests that indigenous peoples were probably better informed than their modern-day descendants about the benefits of enlightened self- interest, which dictated that one should not see inter-group relations as a zero-sum game.

We can also extract building blocks from our core values, sage philosophy and aphorisms. Hence, the Yoruba "omoluabi" model, which rested on civic education right from the cradle, the Igbo concept of "igwebuike," which encapsulated the virtue of cooperation, and societal opprobrium against anti-social behaviour, such as greed (which the Yoruba express as "anikanjopon,""wobia,""jegudujera,""kenimani,""ere ajepajude,""eni kan ku je ki ilu fe"), injustice and oppression, should be woven into the tapestry of our public culture. But the foregoing cannot be done in the absence of leadership, a critical element in the new developmental culture we are proposing. However, that leadership culture also cannot operate in isolation. It is a siamese twin of the developmental state. One such example is the immediate past ruler of Qatar.

The Qatari Challenge

Although the contexts are different, the transformation of Qatar from an oil-rich but underdeveloped wasteland into regional and global recognition in just eighteen years is a big lesson for Nigerian leaders. It may be argued that the autocratic monarchical system in that tiny Arab counti y does not recommend it for comparison. But Nigerians are know'edgeable enough to know that the Nigerian Presidency is one o. the most powerful and often most despotic in the world. When w have dispensed with facile differences, we can then soberly consider the exploits of Qatari Sheikh Hamad bin Khalifa Al-Thani, who supplanted his father in a bloodless palace coup on 27 June 1995 and abdicated in favour of his son on 25 June 2013. In that interval, he transformed his tiny country from a regional backwater into a regional and global player in the aviation, media and diplomatic realms. His Qatari Dream of a small country with global reach saw the creation from the scratch of Al-Jazeera in 1996 to match the Western giants, especially CNN. He also created Qatar Air, which now ranks among the leading players in the global aviation industry. In global power politics, he used the immense wealth of his country to attain the position of a respected power broker in the Middle East and beyond. Yet, he abdicated in favour of his son, even when he could have continued till he became too infirm to rule, like the typical African ruler, who turns public office into a retirement home.

The Qatari challenge to Nigeria's post-independence leaders is manifold (Barakat, 2012; Peterson, 2013). First, the power of vision- thinking big and seeing beyond the challenges. Second, recourse to cultural branding, which is elaborated below. Third, appreciating the true worth of wealth as an enabler of development, which translates to power and influence. This was reflected in policy projection through the deployment of "soft power" and an alliance with the

United States while pursuing an independent foreign policy. The tiny country steadily established a reputation for brokering deals between sworn enemies, hosting strategic peace conferences and building bridges across various divides. Fourth, economic diversification - reducing over-dependence on oil and gas revenues; expansion of the tourism, steel and petrochemical industries; privatization and institution of an investor-friendly regulatory environment - and strategic worldwide investment of its huge revenues from the mainstay oil and gas sector. (Barakat, 2012: 5) Qatar acquired major stakes in key British enterprises (Barclay's Bank, the Sainsbury supermarket chain, London Stock Exchange and Harrods); German and Swiss enterprises - Volkswagen, Porsche, Horchetief AG and Credite Suisse; Singapore's Raffles Hotel; real estate mega projects in London and invested a billion Euros in France, including majority holding in the leading football club. These investments represent "a sound economic policy of recycling oil and gas income into future income streams,' while also spreading "awareness of Qatar's financial strength" and reinforcing its brand as "an international economic force." (Peterson, 2013:2). Fifth, following through to actualization regardless of scepticism and lack of local precedent. Finally, putting country first, such as his voluntary abdication even in the absence of health challenges or apparent intra-dynastic tensions.

As difficult, expensive and time-consuming as it was to brand a country, the Qataris succeeded in carving a niche for themselves through careful and sustained cultural and sports branding. (Barakat, 2012; Peterson, 2013) It was not only targeted at the outside world but it was made to serve a domestic purpose:"fostering a sense of national identity, loyalty and social cohesion." (Barakat, 2012: 9) They pursued the following initiatives: the Qatar Foundation for Education, Science and Community Development; the annual Qatar Cultural Festival; creating a spectacular Museum of Islamic Art as well as museums of history, textiles, photography and modern art; establishing the Al-Jazeera satellite television network, with its global reach; developing a globally competitive

4 "Soft power" has been described as "the ability to appeal to and persuade others,
using the attractiveness of a country's culture, political ideal and policies."
(Barakat, 2012: 7, citing Nye, 2004)

airline and creating an Education City in which local campuses of leading American universities, branch offices of the Rand Corporation, the Brookings Institution and the Royal United Services Institute, were sited; hosting regional and global sporting events, including golf and lawn tennis tournaments and motor racing, culminating in a successful bid to host the 2022 FIFA World Cup. In effect, Qatar has branded itself as "a cultural and intellectual hub through hosting world-renowned academic and cultural centres." (Barakat, 20 12:7)

Shaikh Al-Thani's dramatic reign poses a question: What is the single Big Idea of the Nigerian leadership since independence? As a Nigerian newspaper columnist admonished: "All transformational political elites have a firm vision of where they want to take their countries and how they are going to get there." (Tatalo Alamu, 2013:3) This is a Nigerian chimera.

In spite of three cycles of oil boom and fortuitous windfalls, no single leader, not even those who presided over the windfalls - Generals Gowon, Babangida and Obasanjo - thought of burying the power sector incubus, optimizing the potential of flared natural gas for domestic consumption, running electric-powered railway transport services across the country or creating a globally competitive national carrier in the aviation and maritime transport sectors. Having been nurtured in a culture that is defeatist and incapable of dreaming big, our leaders produced a rat out of the elephant of our natural and human resources. Going farther afield, our leaders have allowed the Nigerian National Petroleum Corporation (NNPC) to remain mired in gross failure, operating as a conduit pipe of patronage while Malaysi's PETRONAS and Brazil's PETROBRAS in similar conditions have built world acclaimed architectural wonders (which have not been torched in the Nigerian treatment of NNPC offices) and become formidable global players in the oil and gas sector.

Bridging the Diversity-Development Divide: Lessons from Penang[5]

As indicated in an earlier passage, Penang is the most ethnically diverse of the States in Malaysia. Yet, it has managed to harness diversity to promote peaceful co-existence and societal development. The following is an outline of some of the principles underlying the Penang experience, based upon a 21-point resolution adopted in Penang at a Roundtable on Cultural Vibrancy. The Resolution articulated the elements of Penang's "Cultural Vibrancy and Diversity," anchored on "a culture of peaceful coexistence" and "living in harmony with the environment.' (Nadarajah, 2002: 3) The ones that are applicable to Nigeria are outlined below.

1. A heritage-conscious society that consolidates its artistic and cultural traditions, the government of which conserves and promotes heritage not only to attract tourists but also for cultural education and inspiration of its peoples.
2. A culturally confident society whose people, young and old, do not suffer from "cultural cringe," that is, an inferiority complex towards foreign cultures that are deemed superior.
3. A people-centred society in which ordinary people matter and their traditions and sacred places are treasured.
4. An enlightened society that values local history, people- centred history and the history of minority and marginalized peoples.
5. A state and society that promotes diversity by protecting the cultural rights of minorities to self-assertion and the coexistence of multiple indigenous languages.
6. A culturally mature society that promotes the expansion of shared values and spaces, and the common heritage of the country's ethnic and religious communities.

[5] This section is heavily reliant on, and paraphrases, Nadarajah, 2002:4-5.

7. A state and society partnership that promotes climatically and culturally appropriate housing (as

opposed to modern 'uglytechture'), with due allowance for greenery, urban quality and open spaces.

8. A culturally vigorous society that absorbs modern technology and modernity to strengthen and diversify its own culture, without subjecting local culture to erosion or obliteration by the forces of globalization.

9. A culturally developed society in which local artistic creativity can be promoted through the support of the public and private sector cultural infrastructure and "infostructure.

10. A culturally discerning society that values authenticity above pastiche, favours the creative rather than the commercial, and supports local creativity to appropriately engage modernity and globalization.

11. A healthy youth culture that flourishes in an atmosphere of ample opportunities for expression, recreation and friendship.

12. An educational system that encourages critical thinking, innovation and creativity, builds character and encourages students to be environmentally sensitive.

13. A reading and information culture, characterized by modern libraries, publishing outlets and literary activities.

14. A resourceful society that develops indigenous knowledge, cultural resources and traditional skills.

15. A culturally concious society that privileges culturally appropriate best practices in ecological, social and economic sustainability.

16. A gender conscious society that pursues pro-women policies for social and gender equity.
17. A historically dynamic society that consciously reinvests in social cultural capital, strengthening cultural institutions to cope with the social and economic challenges of the future.
18. A culturally, socially and environmentally attractive society that promotes and rewards excellence without discrimination.

The foregoing provides useful guidelines for articulating a developmental public culture for Nigeria. Though the citizens of Penang were critical to the evolution and practice of a culture of peaceful co-existence and the use of culture to foster development, their societal initiative was complemented by the role of local and national leadership. This pro-development leadership deficit has bedevilled Nigeria till date and needs to be addressed in the final section of this lecture.

Nigeria: The Imperative of Visionary Leadership and the Developmental State

Just as glue binds separate objects, the link between the reality of diversity and the aspiration of development is leadership. As already well known, leadership deficit is a major disaster that has befallen post-independence Nigeria, and it seems to be a component of our anti-developmental culture, as already indicated. What Nigeria needs to bridge this chasm is the leadership that can envision, strategize and actualize. America had its American Dream, China under Xijing Ping now talks of the Chinese Dream. Now is the time for the Nigerian Dream but it will take a peculiar type of leadership and a particular character of State - a Democratic, Developmental State - to get there.

The admonition of Klaus Vaclav, President of the Czech Republic, who led his people to victory in the Czechoslovak Velvet Revolution," is worth recommending to Nigerian leaders. First, "any large-scale societal change is a *domestic task* because democracy and market economy are not export commodities. They are a do-it yourself project." (Vaclav, 2005). Second, transformation is a sequence of policies, not a once-for-all policy change. Third, transformation, liberalization, deregulation and privatization impose huge costs, which the people must be informed about in advance. Fourth, societies and economies in transition remain fragile and vulnerable for some time. Fifth, the new challenges posed by globalization require "a strong and efficiently functioning state ... which limits its functions to the provision of public goods, to the internalization of externalities, and to helping of people, who are - for various reasons - not able to successfully participate in the market process." (Vaclav, 2005) Finally, "good governance" is not the result of a single reform act but results from an evolutionary process.

The leadership Nigeria needs to break through must be bold, visionary, self-sacrificing and committed to leaving a worthy legacy. The country can no longer afford to be led by megalomaniacs who are overwhelmed by the glamour of office, consumed by their self-importance, fixated on the next "do or die" elections or another term in office while leaving undone urgent tasks of infrastructure development. We need to dispense with so-called leaders who focus on skirmishes and retrograde distractions at the expense of the war on poverty, systemic corruption, erosion of values and the depreciation of the national brand.

Leadership and succession should not be left to chance, the Nigerian way. There must be systematic training in leadership right from the secondary school level, with a heavy dose of national and comparative history spiced with biographies of model leaders.' Nigeria needs an aristocracy of talent in leadership positions, selected by achievement rather than ascription. That select group in all sectors of society must imbibe the new national developmental culture and be steeped in the histories of Nigerian peoples. No nation can develop beyond the knowledge and teaching of its history, a subject that shortsighted Nigerian leaders have taken off the junior secondary school syllabus.

Much has been written on the concept of the Developmental State (Amuwo, 2008, 2010) and the details do not concern us here.[7] What is important to stress is that the Developmental State was the weapon employed by the so-called Asian Tigers in their rise to greatness. The *raison d'etre* of the Developmental State is "to foster a rapid process of capital accumulation, industrialisation and massive investments in social infrastructure and human capital.' (Amuwo, 2010:2). The process is driven by an enlightened and patriotic elite that defines the public/national interest in a way that appeals to a cross-section of society, 'whose members readily embrace and support it. This presupposes that the elite itself must have reached a consensus on what it defines as the national interest and how to achieve it in the interest of the vast majority. A strong sense of nationalism is the key driving force behind the Developmental State and its projects. Meiji Japan, perhaps the oldest modern exemplar of the developmental state, was propelled by the rallying cry of its elite, the self-styled genro: "sonno joi," and "fukoku kyohei" - meaning "rich country, strong military." Accordingly, the "ideology of developmentalism" becomes the weapon that the State deploys in taming capital, guiding, directing and using the market to achieve specific national goals. Realizing that it cannot do without the market, the Developmental State blends the public and private sectors of the economy and aligns market values with social values. A successful Developmental State, it has been asserted, is "a market economy but hardly a market society." (Amuwo, 20 10:2)

As we approach the 2015 Elections, it is important to challenge our political, intellectual, bureaucratic, business, social and religious leaders to ponder the future of the Nigerian State. The need to build a consensus around the core issue of development and the overall goal of improving the lives of the majority of the people in an ordinarily resource-rich country ravaged by corruption, insecurity,

[6] This writer initiated The Caleb Leadership Academy for students of Caleb
  University Imota, Lagos State, soon after assuming office as Vice-Chancellor in
  late 2010. The initiator and selected guest speakers feature on that platform.
[7] The latest issue oftheAfrican Governance Institute (A GI,) Newsletter, No. 40, July
  2013 is a collection of the leading essays on the subject. See,

http://wwv.iagagi.org/spip/IMG/pdf/AGI-Newsetter-N40.pdf,accessed 4 August
  2013.

poor infrastructure and poverty is more urgent than ever. Our leaders must think of how to propel us from the country's current prostrate position. Some practical suggestions can be considered.

1. Apply the selection method of the country's football team, the Super Eagles, to the composition of the cabinet and other key drivers of the government. That is, select our 'First Eleven" regardless of ethnicity, religion and politics. Let Federal Character and Quota System go on recess while we build a country for all.
2. Adopt asymmetrical federalism, which privileges the so-called minorities in holding sensitive positions since they are not likely to be accused of wanting to dominate. The Presidency of the Senate and Chief of Army Staff, for example, may, by general consensus, be ceded to very competent persons from any of the identified groups.
3. Respect the sanctity of the ballot box and defend the people's right to choose their own leaders - no matter how stupid we think those leaders are - and the right to replace them at the next opportunity.
4. Make equity and the welfare of the people our battle cry. That way, we may be on our way to the proverbial Promised Land.
5. Finally, transform the central government by devolving power to the regions. It worked in the First Republic and it has worked in Spain and Canada. Local problems are best solved at the local level by people who live there and are accountable to their own people. Experience has shown that an overly powerful

and oppressive central government is a threat to peace and stability.

Conclusion

President, sir, in this lecture we have advanced two central arguments. First, that diversity as such is not the cause of Nigeria's underdevelopment. Second, that in spite of the ethno-linguistic fragmentation in the country, there is a supra-national anti- developmental culture that drives bad governance and a poor sense of civic responsibility, and that this has been the real threat to national development, unity and the people's well-being. Finally, this lecture draws on the elements in our indigenous history and culture, and practices in other parts of the world to suggest the possibilities of a counter-culture that is developmental, humane and fair.

It submits that a better Nigeria is possible if Nigerian history is taught in schools as a compulsory subject to equip citizens with a sound knowledge of the society that they may have to govern some day in future and whose peoples they must understand and interact with; and if the right kind of leadership could evolve, imbibe and promote a civil, developmental culture. These are given imperatives for the evolution of the right kind of leadership that is imbued with patriotism and capable of promoting a civil and developmental culture. In effect, a new leadership culture must be developed practically from the cradle.

It is only by doing this that the gulf between diversity and development can be bridged by an educated, enlightened and patriotic leadership that can galvanize the people through the agency of a democratic, inclusive, developmental state. Such leaders must be able to invent the Nigerian Dream, an articulated vision of a nation held together by the fibres and sinews of our cultural links, the muscle of our human and natural resources, the backbone of criss-crossing physical and social infrastructure, and the blood of social justice and good governance. If such a leadership could emerge, even in the face of daunting odds, if there is devolution to the regions, and if the famed federal might is applied to solving national problems, and not used as feral might to oppress and impoverish, then, the Nigerian centenary could well lead to the Nigerian century.

References

Ajayi, J. F. Ade and Bashir Ikara (eds.), *Evolution of Political Culture in Nigeria*, Ibadan: University Press Limited.

Akinyele, Rufus Taiwo. 2013. *Lines and Space in Human Affairs: Minorities and Marginals,* University of Lagos Inaugural Lectures Series, Lagos: University of Lagos Press.

Amuwo, Adekunle. 2010. "The Developmental State Instrumentalities and their Relevance to the Discourse on Socio-Economic Challenges in Africa," AISA Policy Brief (African Institute of South Africa), 12, February, 1-8.

Amuwo, Adekunle. 2008. *Constructing the Democratic Developmental State in Africa: A Case Study of Nigeria,* 1960-2007, Occasional Paper No. 59, Johannesburg: Institute for Global Dialogue.

Bates, Robert. 2000. "Ethnicity and Development in Africa: A Reappraisal,"*American Economic Review*, 90(2), 131-134.

Barakat, Sultan. 2012. *The Qatari Spring: Qatar's Emerging Role in Peacemaking,* Kuwait Programme on Development, Governance and Globalisation in the Gulf States, 24, London: London School of Economics and Political Science. Accessed at: http://www.lse.ac.uk/LSEKP/, 25 June 2013.

Bin Saniman, Mohamed Rais. 2008. "Fifty Years of Merdeka: The Role of the New Economic Policy (NEP) in Building a United Malaysian Nation in Diversity." Accessed at: http://bigdogdotcom.wordpress.com/2008/08/10/the-role-of-the-new economic-policy-nep-in-building-a-united-malaysian-nation-indiversity/, 28June 2013.

Collier, Paul and Jan-Wilem Gunning. 1999. "Explaining African Economic Performance, *"Journal of Economic Literature,* 37(1), 64-111.

Easterly, William and Ross Levine. 1997. "Africa's Growth Tragedy: Policies and Ethnic Divisions," *Quarterly Journal of Economics*, 112(4), 1203-1250.

Evers, Hans-Dieter. 2012. "The Value of Ethnic Diversity," Penang Monthly, 31 July. Accessed at: *http://penangmonthly.com/the- value-of-ethnic-diversity/,* 28 June 2013.

Fika, Adamu Muhammed. 1978. *The Kano Civil War and British Overrule*, 1882-1 940, Oxford: Clarendon.

Gören, Erkan 2013. "How Ethnic Diversity Affects Economic Development, *Zentra Working Papers in Transnational Studies*, 14:1-35.
Menon, Jayant. 2008. "Macroeconomic Management Amid Ethnic Diversity: Fifty Years of Malaysian Experience," ADBI Discussion Paper 102. Tokyo: Asian Development Bank Institute,http://www.adbi.org/discussionpaper/2008/04/02/2517.macroeconmic.management.malaysia/, accessed on 28 June 2013.

Montalvo, Jose G. and Marta Reynal-Querol. 2005. "Ethnic Diversity and Economic Development," *Journal of Developing Economics*, 76,293-323.

Nadarajah, M. 2002. '*Cultural Diversity and Sustainability: Preliminary Notes Toward a "Theory" of Penang*,' Paper for the Penang Story International Conference, 18-21 April, Penang, Malaysia.

Nelson, Chijioke. 2013. "How Impunity Slows Nigeria's Development," *The Guardian* (Lagos), 26 June, 21-22.

Nurse, Keith. 2006. "Culture as the Fourth Pillar of Sustainable Development,' Paper Prepared for The Commonwealth Secretariat. London: The Commonwealth Secretariat.

Nye, J. 2004. Soft Power: *The Means to Success in World Politics*. New York:Public Affairs.

O'Connell, James 0. 1967. "The Inevitability of Instability," *Journal of Modern African Studies*, 5(2), 181-191.

Omeihe, Emeka. 2013. "Oguta By-Election: Matters Arising," *The Nation* (Lagos), July 8,22.

Ogunlesi, Tolu. 2013. "Waiting for our Fairy Ship to Dock," *The Punch*, July 8, 25.

Osuntokun, Akinjide and Ayodeji Olukoju (eds). 1997. *Nigerian Peoples and Cultures*, Ibadan: Davidson Press.

Peterson, J.E. 2013. "Qatar's International Role: Branding, Investment and Policy Projection," Policy Brief, Norwegian Peace building Resource Centre, February. Accessed at: http://www.peacebuilding.no, 25 June 2013.

Ranis, Gustav. 2011. "Diversity of Communities and Economic Development: An Overview," Center Discussion Paper 1001, Economic Growth Center, Yale University, September. Accessed at: http://ssrn.com/abstract=1924528, 28 June 2013.

Said, Abdul Aziz. 2004. "Unity in Diversity: The Cultural Mosaic of Iraq," The First Cultural Forum on Iraq, Paris: UNESCO.

Tatalo Alamu. 2013. "The Second Coming of Western Nigeria, *The Nation on Sunday* (Lagos), 30 June, 3.

The Economist (London). 2008. "Qatar: Small Country, Big Ideas," 5 June.

The Economist(London). 2004. "Diversity and Development," 15 July.

The Nation (Lagos). 2013. "Impunity Writ Large," 8 July, 19: Editorial.

UNESCO. 2012. "Culture: A Driver and an Enabler of Sustainable Development," Thematic Think Piece, UN System Task Team on the Post-2015 UN Development Agenda, Paris: UNESCO.

UNESCO, 2010. "Culture for Development Dimesions." Accessed at:
http://www.unesco.org/new/en/culture/themes/cultural diversity/diversity-of-cultural-expressions!programmes/culturefor-developmentindicators/seven-dimensions/, 9 June 2013.

Vaclav, Klaus. 2005. "Qatar Speech: Czech Experience with Radical
Transformation of Society," Speech at Qatar Economic Forum,
Doha, 9 April. Accessed at: http://www.klaus.cz/clanky/581, 25June 2013.

Weaver, Gary. 2008. "The American Cultural Tapestry." Accessed at:
http://iipdigital.usembassy.gov/st/english/publication/2008/05/2008/05/20080528175157xjsnommis0.4013636.html#axzz2X67wP030, 20 June2013.

Williams, Raymond. 1981. *Culture*, Glasgow: Fontana Paperbacks.

Yeoh, Emile Koh-Kheng. 2013. "Socioeconomic Development and Ethn-Cultural Diversity: State Policy and the Evolvement of Pluralism in Malaysia," *International Journal of Business Anthropology*, 4(1), 12 1-143.

Different Climes, Different Bird Songs:
A Peep into Nigeria's Linguistic Tapestry

Professor (Mrs) Eno-Abasi Urua, FNAL

Preamble

Which of dem wego speak?
One metre --
We travel to Umunede, wego speak Isoko,
We travel to Borno, say na Fulfulde,
We travel to Ughelli, dem go speak Urhobo,
We travel to Buguma, say na Kalabari,
We travel to Kaduna, dem go speak Hausa,
We travel to Okene, dem go speak Ebira,
We travel to Abbi, dem go speak Kwale,
Ogornola, dem go speak Okrika,
One kilometre means another language,
half a kilometre means another language,
One metre...
We travel to Sokoto, dem go speak Fulani,
We go to Benin City, dem go speak Edo,
We travel to Onitsha, dem go speak Igbo,
We travel to Asaba-Asa, den Bendel we go,
We travel to Gboko, dem say na Tiv,
We travel to Otukpa, dem go speak Idoma,
We'travel to Akure, dem go speak Yoruba,
We travel to Ase, dem go speak Aboh,
We travel to Uyo, na Ibibio,
We travel, we travel, we travel traveltravel
All I'm saying, Lingua franca...

One metre...
We travel to Patani, dem go speak Izon,

We travel to Vom, dern go speak Berom,
We travel to Ekpoma, dem go speak Esan,
We travel to Auchi, dem go speak Etsako,
We travel to idah, dem go speak Igala,
We travel to Bida, demgo speak Nupe,
We travel to Ogbakiri, dem go speak Ikwere

This popular song, by Evi Edna Ogholi, (taken from Uwe Seibert's website on Language Ecology of Nigeria (accessed Sat June 22, 2013).

1.0   Introduction

"Nigeria's Cultural Tapestry1' is the title of the 2013 Convocation lecture. Tapestry evokes images of woven, beautiful, intricate designs. In Figure 1, we provide a few examples of African tapestry.

Figure 1: Pictorial examples of African tapestry (found and
taken from the Google images)

Characteristically, tapestries are known for their complexities, pictures or stories within pictures, a widening and narrowing mosaic of colour hues, texture, length, depth and width. This title seems to me to be a reflection of the haunting beauty, the complexities that constitute the Nigerian cultural (land)scape. Culture reflects the totality of the way of life of a people, including language and how it is used, religion, agricultural practices, economic activities, politics, social structures and networks, arts, crafts - the tangible ar d intangible aspects of the totality of how a people live. Even from a very cursory look at Nigeria, it seems quite explicit that myriads of cultures can be identified within Nigeria. Nigeria's cultural 'tapestry is a fascinating subject that would cover tomes compiled from serious research intervention and consequently a subject that should be pursued methodically and aggressively.

In this paper, we shall discuss 'Nigeria's cultural tapestry' in the context of Nigeria's linguistic diversity. Nigeria's diversity in all aspects is not in dispute - from the weather, culture, language, politics, religion, economic, science and technology, etc. With very broad strokes, we shall provide a snapshot of the extent of the complex tapestry we are talking about here. Geographically, Nigeria seems to be divided into two by natural features in the Niger and Benue rivers, splitting the country in half, (**some people talk about 'fault lines' and sometime in August 2013 the President, Dr. Goodluck Ebele Jonathan, made an oblique reference to this, and concluded that the country will outlive the pessimists**). Politically, the north is characterized by feudal system of traditional governance, the south west by a kingship system and the eastern component by a rather republican system of traditional governance. Culturally, there is as much variation in the way of life of the people. Achebe(2012:2, 11) summarises the religious tapestry as comprising "animists, muslims and Christians alike held together by a delicate artificial lattice with the older religion in retreat". Culturally and linguistically, we come close to having a parade of sorts.

Given the kaleidoscope of the very complex tapestry that is Nigeria, I plead that for the sake of my sanity and that of this distinguished audience, kindly permit me to restrict myself to some aspects of the linguistic thread of our beautiful if rather complex tapestry.

In addressing this topic, I shall first discuss in a general sense the tapestry as diversities, which shall include the geographical, political, cultural and linguistic composition of that tapestry. Next, I shall zero in on the linguistic diversity starting from the language families to the fascinating characteristics of our languages; we shall take a brief look at how other countries have handled their diversity and then suggest how we can harness this for national integration and development; finally, we shall consider the outlook and conclusion.

The importance of language cannot be overemphasized - in one instance, it has been suggested that language is life (Urua 2007).Language is an extremely crucial aspect of a people's cultural heritage. Through language one can understand the social structures and networks embedded in a society. Language provides an access to the way a people think and therefore a means to understand how people respond to similar or different situations (Sapir Whorf hypothesis). This partially explains why coloniserstarget the era dication of the colonized people's language, replace it with theirs, in order to control and manipulate the way the people think and subsequently act. Of course, there are counterexamples, a familiar one being the Fulanis and Hausas in Nigeria (see Elugbe 1992/2011). Language is a means of forming identities at different levels.

2.0 Diversity in Nigeria

The vastness of Nigeria is underscored with a land area of91 0,77 1 sq km and a total area of 923,768 sq km. Her neighbours are the republic of Niger to the north, Chad republic to the north east, Cameroon to the east, Benin Republic o the west, and the Gulf of Guinea to the south. The import of this information is to underscore the linguistic diversity and cross border languages which impinge on pluralistic tendencies aid activities in Nigeria and Africa.

Geopolitically, Nigeria consists of thirty-six states, divided into six groupings, viz., North West, North East, North Central, South West, South East and South South and the Federal Capital Territory in Abuja. (Currently in the Nigerian polity, there is a strident clamour for the creation of more states before the expiration of the fifth republic!).Akhough it is possible to merge the three northern zones to form one northern block and to merge the three South zones to also form one southern block, each of these geopolitical groupings in itself, is rich with a wide diversity of culture. Figure 2 shows the political map of Nigeria while the geopolitical groupings with the constituent states are presented in Table 1.

Figure 2: Political Map of Nigeria showing the FCT Abuja and the 36 States

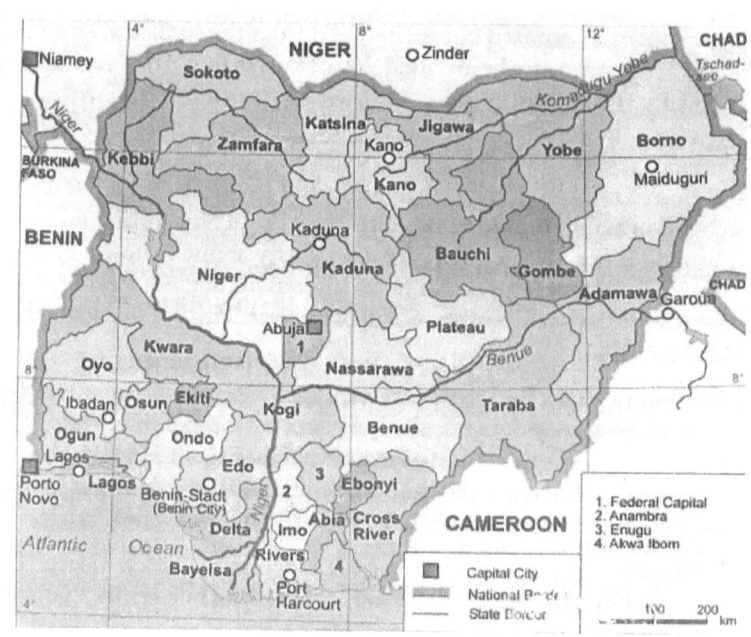

Table 1: Geopolitical Groupings of the 36 States in Nigeria

North Central	North East	North West	South East	South South	South West
Benue	Adamawa	Jigawa	Abia	Akwalbom	Ekiti
Kogi	Bauchi	Kaduna	Anambra	Bayelsa	Lagos
Kwara	Borno	Kano	Ebonyi	Cross	Ogun

				River	
Nasarawa	Gombe	Katsina	Enugu	Delta	Ondo
Niger	Taraba	Kebbi	Imo	Edo	Osun
Plateau	Yobe	Sokoto		Rivers	Oyo
**FCT		Zamfara			

2.1 Geographical Diversity

The country, as pointed out earlier, and from the (political) map in Figure 2, appears to be divided into two parts by the two most important rivers, Niger and Benue, which form a sort of horizontal belt across the country. In terms of the weather, the north is more of savannah - dry, hot and dusty, with less quantity and shorter duration of rainfall of between 508mm and 1524mm (20inches to 60 inches) annually from May to September. From November through February there is the cold, dry and dusty winds known as the harmattan. Temperatures can be as high as 40 degrees Celsius and above in the dry season in the north of Nigeria. Parts of the north are near desert-like.

On the other hand, the south with a tropical rainforest climate is wet nearly all year round, particularly between March and November, with varying degrees of rainfall intensity ranging between 1524mm to 2032mm (60 inches to 80 inches) annually. Nigeria's Niger Delta is said to be one of the largest in the world (http://www.rawdp.org).

Nigeria also has a rich and varied ecosystem, which boasts of fascinating bio diverse flora and fauna including butterflies, such as the rare species in the Cross River region known as *acraea oreas oboti* named in honour of the late Professor Emmanuel Obot who did extensive research on this species; drill monkeys and quite recently a newly discovered gecko species in Cross River and Akwa Ibom States, christened *hemidactylus eniangii*, named after Dr. Edem Eniang of the University of Uyo, Nigeria.

2.2 Linguistic and cultural diversity

According to Ethnologue (www.ethnologue.org), over 500 languages are spoken across Nigeria, reflecting the enormous linguistic diversity of the country. Three of the four language families found in Africa are represented in Nigeria, namely, Niger Congo, Afro Asiatic and Nib Saharan, further underscoring the diversity of the language groupings. While the Niger Congo phylum parades the bulk of languages spoken in Nigeria, about 75%; Afro Asiatic has about a quarter and Nib Saharan has just two to three languages on the Saharan side (http://www.uiowa.edu/intlinet/unijos/nigonnet/nlp/geneti c.htm). The greater percentage of the languages spoken in Nigeria today belongs to the Benue Congo of the Niger Congo phylum. Elugbe (1992/2011) attempts to account for the linguistic diversity that characterizes the Nigerian scape. According to him, "Nigeria falls squarely within the fragmentation belt' (p.19) which is defined by Dalby (1977:6) quoted in Elugbe (1992/2011:18) as 'a zone extending from Senegal to Ethiopia and northern Tanzani'.

2.2.1 Linguistic diversity

What thematically for our purpose is linguistic tapestry, shall be henceforth discussed under linguistic diversity, a more familiar terminology in the linguistic literature. The linguistic diversity of Africa, particularly that of sub-Saharan Africa is not new; in fact the claim has been made that of the approximately 7000 languages worldwide more than one third is found in Africa (www. ethnologue.org). Of that number over a quarter can be found in Nigeria (Seibert, Elugbe 1992/201 1 Attention has often been drawn to the dense linguistic diversity in the West African region, particularly in the area between Nigeria and Cameroon (Nettle, e 1996, 1998, Childs 2003, Connell 2010, Urua 2010, etc.). According d to Brent Consulting, Nigeria is ranked 5th globally in language diversity (http://brenttconsu1ting.wordpress.com/2012/02/24/nigeri a-5th-in-language-diversity/).

But beyond the sheer numbers, some scholars have attempted to account for the reasons for the language density in this region. Nettle (1996) links the number of languages to economic activities and concludes that "ecological risk has been a key historical force in West Africa and that the ethnolinguistic mosaic can be used as a valuable 'fossil record' of people's adaptive social and economic strategies." In a follow up study published in 1998, Nettle ties language diversity with the climate, suggesting that where the climate permits all round food production, people can settle in self- sufficient groups leading to more language diversity.

Nigeria itself is a linguistic labyrinth, a tangle of well over 500 languages (www.ethnologue.org), most of which are "endemic autochthonous", a term I happily borrow from that ardent language activist, ToveSkutnabb-Kangas. Some of the very popular, better known ones are not necessarily the autochthonous but the 'imported' ones such as Arabic and English. We shall however, move away from the numbers to take a look at a few of the fascinating features of these, languages and how as a nation we can make capital (in all its various ramifications) of this tapestry!

This then leads us to the title, a slice of this diversity in discourse. The first part of my title is a rough translation of an Ibibio proverb which says, **'kwa idañ, kwa uyio inuen'**, roughly translated to mean, **'(for) every clime, a different birdsong'!** That to me captures the inherent and natural diversity intended in nature. Differences are recognized and affirmed, neither denigrated nor derided! As distinguished members of the Academy of Letters we recognize and appreciate the intrinsic complex beauty in a country with so many languages, cultures, political, religious, social leanings and different ethnic nationalities. In Figure 3, we illustrate the linguistic diversity with a language map of Nigeria (Crozier & Blench 1992).

Figure 3: Language Map of Nigeria (Crozier & Blench 1992)

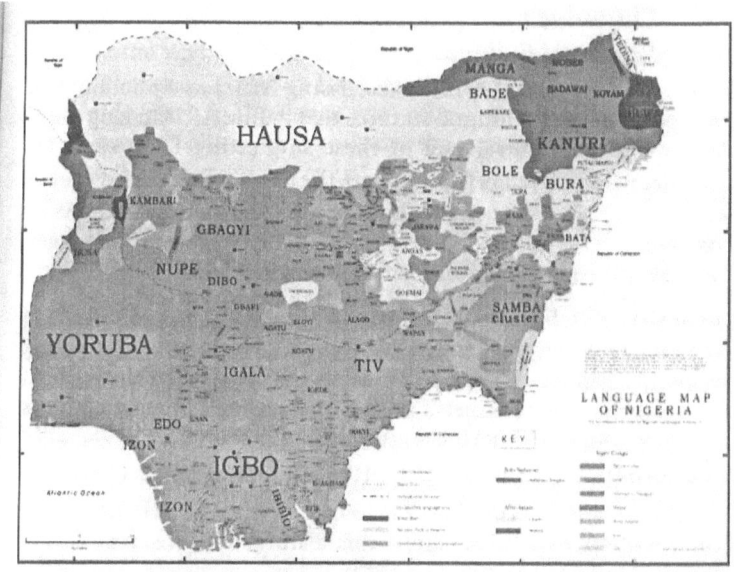

3.0 Fascinating features of Nigerian languages

We shall attempt to take a portrait of some of the fascinating features of just a handful of these languages from a purely linguistic and also from sociolinguistic viewpoints. Because of the breadth, depth and width of the subject matter, it will be impossible to showcase in a short paper such as this, the linguistic/sociolinguistic features of the 500+ Nigerian languages. Rather we shall present samples but make suggestions on how we can unearth the layers of the others not discussed here as well as discover more exciting features, even from the ones mentioned. In order to proceed meaningfully, we shall attempt to explore the subject from different perspectives, viz., segmental, prosodic, grammatical and sociolinguistic aspects of the Nigerian linguistic tapestry. And with my bias in phonology, I shall probably lean more on the linguistic tapestry from that standpoint.

3.1 Phonology

3.1.1 Segmental Features

Clements & Rialland (2005) in discussing Africa as a phonological area, point out some unique features that define African languages. At the segmental level one of these interesting features is the presence of labial-velars [kp, gb, ŋm], the doubly articulated sounds which pose a great challenge for our European and Asian colleagues. This feature is present in many Nigerian languages, including Yoruba, Igbo, Ibibio, to mention just a few!

Implosives which are voiced stops produced without any buildup of air in the oral cavity (Clements & Osu 2002) is another fascinating segmental feature. Hausa, a Chadic language spoken throughout the northern part of Nigeria as first and second languages, attests implosives. In addition Hausa attests ejective sounds.

Although contrastive aspirated stops are not common in African languages, some Nigerian languages, viz., Owerri Igbo and Kohumuno (Cross River) attest this feature. The observation has also been made that one feature that characterizes a number of African languages including Nigerian languages is the paucity of the[p] sound. Yoruba is a good example of a language without the [p1 sound. Even where some Nigerian languages attest the p sound, the distribution is often restricted to weak positions such as final positions or where it is susceptible to weakening and eventual loss (Ibibio and many Lower Cross languages).

Two other features include the prevalence of syllabic nasals. Syllabic nasals are the sole occupants of the syllable in which they occur, e.g., in the word **n.dap** 'dream' (noun)' (Ibibio), [n] which is the syllabic nasal is the only occupant of that syllable. Usually syllabic nasals are homorganic to the following consonant as we see in the n.dap example.

Consonant clusters are rare in Niger Congo languages.

3.1.2 *Prosody*
3.1.2.1 Tone
One of the very fascinating features of many African languages is tone. Nearly all Nigerian languages appear to be tonal, apart from Fulfulde. Back in the day, it was quite common for our European and western colleagues to consider the presence of the tone feature as exotic, whereas to us it is the norm. Welmers (1973:77) mirthfullycaptures the attitude of some linguists when they are confronted with tones in African languages adding that some consider tone as a species of esoteric, inscrutable, an utterly unfortunate accretion characteristic of underprivileged languages - a sort of cancerous malignancy afflicting an otherwise normal linguistic organism." A classic definition of tone is that provided by Pike (1948) as "a language having lexically significant, contrastive, but relative pitch on each syllable." There is no uniformity with respect to the number of tones Nigerian languages have. Greenberg (1983) makes the claim that the predecessor of the Niger Congo family had two basic tones, high and low. However, Nigerian languages vary in the number of tone levels ranging from two to five. Ibibio, Igbo (Benue Congo) have two level tones plus a downstep feature in addition to the rising and

falling contour tones. Yoruba has three level tones, high, mid, and low. Hausa (Chadic) and Mbembe (Cross River) attests five level tones. Lexical and grammatical are some of the functions tone performs in Nigerian languages. We shall consider a few of such examples from some Nigerian languages including, Igbo and Ibibio.

Contrastive Tone (Igbo)
1.   ike   'strength, power'
        ike   'buttocks'

Grammatical Tone (Ibibio)
The grammatical function of tone in the Ibibio languageis very robust. For instance, the grammatical aspect is marked by tonal morphemes. For brevity and simplicity, we shall only present examples of the progressive aspect which is marked by a HL falling tone as indicated on the verbs which have been underlined for ease of identification. Both high and low toned verbs have identical tonal pattern in Ibibio progressive constructions as shown in 2 and 3. The basic verb forms are in parentheses.

2.   **Progressive Aspect (High toned verbs)**
        (se)   eme a se usun   "Eme is looking at the road."
        (yet)   eme ayet ikpan   "Eme is washing (a) spoon."
        (kere)   eme akere ekikere   "Eme is thinking (thought)."

4.   **Progressive Aspect (Low toned verbs)**

        (bo)   eme abo eno   "Eme   is receiving a gift."

(nwan)   eme a nwan iyak   "Eme is drying fish."

(daara)   eme a daara usan.   "Eme is rinsing plate(s).

3.1.2.2   *Tonal Homophones*
Just as there are segmental homophones (site/sight; eye/I; dye/die),tones also can be homophones or "homotones". We provide examples from the Ibibio language, a Lower Cross language spoken in AkwaIbom State. This underscores the autosegmental insight of the autonomy of tones in language.

4.   **Ibibio (Tonal homophone)**
   tem   'cause to sit (e.g. an infant')
   term   'cook'

   sem   'shine
   sem   'speak in a foreign language'

In addition to the tone levels, there is the additional fascinating issue of tonal registers, where identical tones in an utterance may be realized at progressively different lower levels, giving the impression of one descending a flight of steps - this explains the moniker, downstep! This phenomenon is found in many tone languages including Ibibio, Igbo, Hausa, etc. And there is the astonishing feature of floating tones in African (Nigerian) tone languages as well!

3.1.2.3   *Vowel Harmony - Igbo*
Vowel harmony, observed in a number of Nigerian languages, is a phenomenon where all the vowels in a

word are constrained to be from a particular set (Bamgbose on Yoruba, 1967, Carnochan 1960, Green & Igwe 1963 on Igbo). It has also been reported for a number of African languages (Akan: Stewart 1967). This is on account of the advanced and retracted tongue root. We shall illustrate this feature from the Igbo language. In the Igbo language for instance the vowels "are neatly divided into two sets" (Welmers 1973:33), such that only the vowels of a particular set can be found in a word, no cross carpeting!

Table 2: Igbo Vowel Harmony Sets

Set I	Set 2
i	I
e	a
o	ɔ
u	ʊ

Examples
5.   oke 'rat'   aka 'maize'
     okwu 'word'   akwu fire'

Words can contain vowels from only one set as illustrated above in Table 2.

1.1.2.4.1 Intonation

There has been some controversy about whether or not African (Nigerian) languages have a rising intonation pattern for questions, something which has been suggested as having its base from I western European languages, particularly English. Evidence from research on other languages other than Germanic or Indo-European has shown varied intonation patterns. Hausa (Chadic) and Oro (Lower Cross) indubitably have sentence final rise intonation pattern. Isoko has a final lowering or a falling intonation. Nupe (Benue Congo) on the other hand has final lengthening as a question marker. Other languages (Ibibio) seem to have no overt pitch raising as far as questions are concerned. Time and space will not permit us to explore other phonological features such as nasalization, vowel length, segment deletion, gemination, etc.

3.2 Morphology and Syntax
3.2.1 Reduplication
Languages find a number of creative ways to be productive in terms of word formation, sentence structure, etc. Reduplication is a process where a portion or the entire word is copied onto the stem to form another word with different though semantically related meanings. This has been reported for many Nigerian languages (Ibibio, Leggbo, etc.). Reduplication may be partial or total. We present data from Leggbo, an Upper Cross subgroup of Cross River group spoken in Abi and Yakurr Local Government Areas of Cross River State to illustrate both partial and total reduplication. Lexical items such as nouns and verbs show partial reduplication - nouns to mark diminutive forms while verbs are reduplicated to indicate intensity. We illustrate with examples 6 to 12 taken from Udoh (2004, 2007).

3.2.1.1   *Partial Reduplication*

Nouns

6. itobo 'monkey'
   ito-tobo-we 'small monkey'
   ito-tobo-be 'small monkeys'

7. lete-bbol 'heart'
   lete-bbo-bbo-we 'small heart
   lete-bbo-bbo-be 'small hearts'

Verbs

8. du 'beat'
   du-du 'really beat'

9. mina 'lie down'
   mi-mina 'really lie down'

10. yei-gekwe 'rest'
    ye-yei-gekwe 'really rest'

3.2.1.2   Total Reduplication
Total reduplication is used to mark plurality in Leggbo grammar. For instance,

11. esi kkpem 'black bag'
    esi kkpem kkpem 'black bags'

12. lettol ggbɔi 'long head'
    lettol ggbɔi ggbɔi 'long heads'

3.2.2   Serial Verbs
At the syntactic level, serial verbs (verb serialization) present a very interesting aspect of linguistic research both to the native and nonnative speakers. Many Nigerian languages attest serial verbs, where verbs in a clause are piled one after another into a string

without any auxiliaries or conjunctions. Many scholars have devoted a lot of energy to theoretical and analytical implications of serial verb constructions (Bamgbose 1974, 1982, Awobuluyi1973, and Lawal 1989 for Yoruba). Examples from Yoruba(Lawal 1989):

13. Ayo ju   iwe mo   Kọla
    Ayo threw book stick Kọla
    'Ayo threw the book at Kola'
14. Bọla wa   ẹgbọn   rẹ   lo   ẹkọ
    Bọla search elder sister/brother her go   Lagos
    'Bola went to search for her elder sister/brother in Lagos'

3.2.3 Ideophones

Ideophones are features of African which hold much fascination for language scholars. They have been reported for Igbo, Yoruba, Ibibio, Leggbo, etc. According to Cole (1955), the ideophone is "often onomatopoeic, which describes a qualificative, predicative or adverb with respect to sound, color, smell, manner, state, action or intensity". Ideophones can be classified into different word classes depending on how they function in the particular language. In Leggbo, ideophones are more robust since they perform a number of grammatical functions. Udoh (2007:5 8) reports that "they modify the grammatical categories that express processes, states and nouns", specifically of the adverbial and adjectival functions. Ideophones have no fixed structure - they can be monosyllabic, polysyllabic, reduplicated, etc. Again we provide examples from Udoh (2007:59):

15. esi ffai   ffai'whitebagst
    bagwhite.IDEO   Redup

16. e-de kkaNN   it is hard'
     it-is hard.IDEO

3.2.4 Logophors - Uda (Lower Cross)

Lower Cross languages have been shown to attest reflexive pronouns and reflexivisation. In addition, logophoric pronouns are also attested. These are pronouns which refer to the fact that the subject of another clause is identical as that of the preceding clause. Logophors are usually found in storytelling and in reported speech. We illustrate with the following examples taken from Uda, a Lower Cross language spoken in Akwalbom State:

17. o-koke ani ɔbɔk a-kaka oyo ɔ-nɔ imɔ ididip ibi
     3SGPro-said that the monkey 3SGPro-held child
     3SGPro- give 3SGLOG 3SGPro-enable weed
     'She said that the monkey babysat for me, which enabled me to weed
18. Efretei o-ko ki imɔ inyoŋ
     PN   3rdPro-sayCOMP 3SGLOG leave
     'Efretei said he left.

Notice that the reflexive here is im? rather than aŋi for the 3rd singular pronoun. This variation applies to the 1st person plural in the reported reference. We illustrate in table 3 below:

Table 3: Comparison of Independent and Logophoric forms

	Independent/ Subject	Logophoric Form Form	Gloss (English)

1 Sg.	Ami	im	I
1Pl.	ŋnn	mmim/ndim	We

3.2.5 Gender in Hausa

Gender is used distinctively in Hausa. The World Atlas for Language Structures (www.wals.info) states that the 'Niger Congo family is the major source' of gender languages and so provides patterns for gender distinction in independent personal pronouns in Hausa. Illustrations in the Atlas are taken from Newman 2000:477. A

19.

1SGni		1PLmu	
2SGM.	kai	2PLku	
2SGF.	ke		
3SGM.	shi	3SGM.su	
3SGF.	ita		

3.2.6 Noun Class in Efik

Many Benue Congo languages are noted for having nouns which are classified based on semantic features. It could be on the basis of number, gender (Hausa), size, texture, colour, etc. We provide examples from Efik(Lower Cross) taken from Welmers (1973).

20.	**Noun**		**Adj + Noun**	
	bja	'yam'	akaniabja	'old yam'
	bud	'shame'	akambaobud	'great
	bjɔŋ	'hunger'	Akamba ɔbiɔŋ	shame'

			'great hunger'

3.3   Language Use in Society

Beyond the purely linguistic features attested in Nigerian languages, are crosscutting issues that straddle how language interfaces with society. Chinua Achebe describes proverbs as the palm oil with which words are eaten in the African context. Proverbs are unique in that they are interspersed with normal discourse for didactic purposes. Even within genres, diversity abounds. Although it is a fact that most African languages make profuse use of proverbs mainly for instructive purposes, some proverbs are purely manipulated for entertainment and insult. The manipulation of tone is used in many Nigerian languages to perform various kinds of entertainment. Many Nigerian languages such as Yoruba and Ido ma, for instance, adopt a complex use of tone and drum music (Arrstrong 1954). There is documentation for puns, tone and erotic tone riddles found in Lower Cross languages and popularized by Donald Simmons in a series of publication between the 1950s and 1960s. We provide examples of some tone riddles from the Ibibio language:

3.3.1 Tone riddles in Ibibio

21.

Call: ekpu kwuOt kwuO taduk usuN nto (L-H L-L H-!H H-H H-L)
Response: uso (a)men usuN asio ndOt enyen (L-H L- L H- !H H-H H-L

Call: OkOOk ufiOn, ebre ufiOn, abre afo asaNa die OdOOk OkOOk *Response:*   enyON tlk, abasi tlk, abasi afoasaNa die adidad owo

Call: ituud OkpO usuN asaN aadimuk
Response: anana ayineka asana adiyo

Call: ikpON ibitte akuurn adia
Response: owo umaaha asikke akpere

Call: emum usasak eyaak enim ekiibuN mba
Response: ekop etighi ye usuN ke itON nyrOk

3.3.2 Gender based language variation

In the Ubang community in Obudu Local Government Area of Cross River State where the language spoken is also known as Ubang, it has been reported that there is gender based language variation with respect to language use in the same household. Children grow up speaking the mother tongue', literarily but from about age 5, the male children learn and begin to speak the adult male language while the girls learn and begin to speak the adult women language: We provide a few lexical items and sentences taken from Ibli(1998: 104):

Table 4: Examples of gender based language variation in Ubang

Female variety	Male variety	Gloss
Lexical items		
Bachu	Batu	Palm wine
Nnse	Nnche	Boy
Okwuri	Nkuri	Maize
Kangwim	Kangwum	Bird
Ukakwe	Kobu	Dog
Kirui	Ketong	Yam

Ariga	Nki	Dress
Ugbala	Nko	Cup
Ushanne	Ribuo	Playground
Sentences		
ariga aye akpum	nkionyeokpum	My dress is dirty
ukakweobuu	kobukaonea	The dog has run away
chon me	buu me	

Although Ubang is a tone language and reference has actually been made to differences possibiy based on 'some tonal variation', tone was not marked in the source where I obtained the data (Ibli 1998: l(4-1O5). The genth'r based variation in the language is based on the intercultural and intermarriage between women and men from the neighbouring communities who have different languages (Ibli 1998; personal communication with Dr. Joseph Ushie who is an indigene of the area). This differentiation, it is claimed, will be sustained because each gender conscious y reinforces its speech form in order to maintain the status quo! 'This may be instructive for language maintenance.

In the above section, we have showcased just a few of the fascinating features found in Nigerian languages. The next section shall touch on some of the challenges.

4.0   Challenges
Depending on one's perspective, linguistic diversity or multilingualism can be viewed as an asset and a blessing; rather than as a liability and a curse. Although Nigeria is a very diverse country in more ways than one - the flora, the fauna, the weather, the topography, the people, the religion - the culture and the many languages spoken on its shores, attest to the immense diverse colours of the

Nigerian space. National planners may tend to have a rather negative view of multilingualism and diversity in Nigeria and blame the challenges faced in nation building on the fact of diversity and multilingualism. A critical assessment of such a position shows that such a charge can hardly be justified (see also Elugbe 1992/2011).

From the much we have seen, our languages consist of bundles of fascinating and complex tapestries on account of the unique and mesmerizing features and information they pack. Our languages contain information about our knowledge systems including our ecology, history, law and order, environment/geography, religion, culture, health/medicine, sanitation and so much more. Our languages have contributed significantly to our understanding of how language functions in a generic sense. Studies on the Efik syllable structure (Clements 1983) partly contributed to Hyman's theory of syllable weight and Goldsmith's (1980) seminal work on autosegmental theory was as a direct result of his research on Igbo tones. We can also use our languages to great advantage in the tourism industry. I often illustrate how language can tell us so much about a people with the story of fellow graduate student from the Republic of Cameroon in the University of Ibadan in 1990.   He was surprised that my language has a word which is equivalent to the English word 'div' since his language did not. I come from the riverine area with large bodies of water whereas he came from the grasslands in Cameroon. 1a

Quite apart from the numbers, the absence of a clearly defined m language policy, as well as the internal and external threats to our H languages leading to language endangerment, I am convinced that sh the greater challenge is the fact that most of our languages remain cc undocumented and undescribed. The implication is that we lose a much of the knowledge embedded in our communities through h language loss. Today, we have witnessed the aggressive interest of western scholars passionately espousing language documentation, whose aim "is to provide a comprehensive record of the linguistic practices characteristic of a given speech community" the linguistic practices consists of "the observable linguistic behavior m and the native speakers' metalinguistic knowledge" (Himmelmann la 1998). The idea of 'comprehensive' sounds invasive and it seems n invasive because we observe that nothing is spared - from private a conversations, the ecology, flora and fauna, local knowledge and re technology systems, etc. And communities are made to sign in agreements to permit the publication and assess to the data so hi collected. The data are rarely stored in local archives but rather in Europe/America/Asia, etc. Western funding agencies fund these projects. This should be a source of concern to us because, perhaps sooner than later, we may not be able to access some of the plants, especially if they have medicinal or commercial value since we may N have signed away our rights.

Having said that, it is absolutely crucial for us to document and describe every aspect of our language and culture for posterity, for the inherent knowledge in our cultures and languages, for research, for pedagogy, for tourism, etc. Documentation is here to stay, regardless of the motives. There are available today technological tools that can assist us in the rapid documentation of our languages a and culture, from our smart phones, iPads, audio and video equipment, the blog spots, internet, Facebook, YouTube, Instagram, etc. But beyond the high tech end of language documentation, nothing prevents us from documenting our languages and culture with the tried and trusted traditional methods of notebook and pen/pencil, photographs, etc.

However, we need funding in order to have a critical mass given the sheer numbers we are talking about here -500 languages and counting! Some of us have benefitted from funding from external agencies but we have also undertaken many other projects that have been funded from personal resources and the goodwill of family and friends. I also am aware that many Nigerians who are very passionate about their cultures and languages have invested huge personal resources in the documentation of their languages and culture. But these activities have neither been systematic, methodological nor coordinated. Training people to engage in language documentation using modern technological tools is a necessity. Qualified and skilled manpower ensures that with availability of funding, quality work is assured. Consider this reaction of a colleague in response to a paper written by a neophyte in historical linguistics on a Nigerian language group and sent to him for consideration:

> *"I was sent the attached paper on Bette-Bendi, which is the usual mixture of interesting and slightly bizarre. What people could do f they were properly trained!"*

NAL could persuade the various levels of government on the wisdom of investing in Nigerian languages given the enormous capital that can be made out of our rich cultural tapestry in tourism, employment, etc. Therefore our various levels of government, beginning with the Federal should annually set aside (substantial) funds for the systematic and urgent documentation of our cultural heritage. I come from a community where we cherish quality food and so we have a saying that goes, **efere enemde ŋkpɔ akpa atak** - when the sauce tastes delicious, it must of necessity cost something. We must provide substantial resources for research into our rich linguistic and cultural tapestry. The significant injection of funds into the documentation and subsequent development of our languages will go a long way in training and building capacity, acquisition of the tools necessary for language documentation, setting up of local cultural and language archives where the products from such projects are stored for easy accessibility to the local community and other interested parties. Language diversity is by no means peculiar to Nigeria. We shall now briefly consider how two countries have managed their diversities.

5.0   Managing linguistic diversity elsewhere
In terms of diversity, Nigeria is by no means unique, but perhaps from the point of view of the sheer number of diverse groups and languages located within one geopolitical space, Nigeria may be very visible. Many more countries have diverse populations and manage them for the overall optimal benefit of their people. We shall take a quick look at two countries with diversity one in Africa and the other in Asia, and hopefully learn a few lessons on how they have successfully managed diversity for national integration and development.

My take on this year's theme addresses how linguists can work with everyone, including students, community members, language aficionados, and the government to exploit the benefits of linguistic diversity in Nigeria for national integration and development.

5.1   South Africa

With a population of a little over 47.9 million, consisting of a mosaic population of Africans, Europeans, Coloured people and Asians, South Africa has the sobriquet of a 'rainbow' state, underscoring its diverse composition; the multi-coloured South African flag is a symbolic representation of that diversity. It does seem that there is no attempt to pretend that South Africa is a homogenous entity. But how does it deal with the different peoples, languages and cultures? The South African government recognises 11 official languages, viz., Zulu, Afrikaans, English, Ndebele, Swati, Northern Sotho, Southern Sotho, Xhosa, Tswana, Tsonga and Venda (Brenzinger, 1997). With the recognition of the eleven official languages, the South African government set up a Language Task Group aka LANGTAG committee in 1996 "to produce a framework for the development of a comprehensive national language policy" (Webb, 2002). These eleven languages serve the language needs of the different linguistic groups in South Africa at different levels. Of course, this does not suggest that all the languages serve equal functions. The crucial thing is that the languages are recognised and accorded relevance.

5.2   Sri Lanka

Sri Lanka, with over 19 million people, recognises two main languages, namely, Sinhala and Tamil (official and national). Other languages used in the country include

English, (10%), Indo-Portuguese, Sri Lankan Creole Malay, Sri Lankan Sign Language, Veddah (www.ethnologue.org). Having had a history of civil upheaval and conflict and having understood the significance of language to national reconciliation, integration and development, Sri Lanka has established a full-fledged Ministry of National Languages and Social Integration. Indeed, support for this position, or should one say conviction, comes from evidence from the vision and mission statements of the Ministry and pronouncements by the President of Sri Lanka and key officials.

From the official website of the Ministry, http://lanintegmin.govJk, we extract a few quotations as follows,

> *The Ministry of National Languages and Social Integration, established in April 2010, has a pivotal role to play in a post conflict era where the people of Sri Lanka are looking forward to the fresh dawn of a prosperous tomorrow.*
> *We are deeply committed to the noble task of facilitating all the communities to live in peace and harmony in a country enlivened by the colours of diversity while ensuring the language rights enshrined in the Constitution.*

Vision statement
> *A unified Sri Lankan nation celebrating unity in endearingly intertwined by two languages ensuring the identity of all communities.*

Mission statement

Policy formulation, guidance and facilitation to create a developed and socially integrated trilingual society that assures rights of and all and respects each other.

Message from the President of Sri Lanka
"Protection of the rights of the economically and socially disadvantaged groups and improvement of their living conditions will be given high priority with a view to ensuring their active participation in socio-economic activities."

Message from the Minister
"The Ministry of National Languages and Social Integration was established with a view to enhance the freedom of communities, communal harmony, strong understanding , Religious and Cultural bonds, and develop a society with equal opportunities for every citizen of this country."

Message from the Secretary
"The primary objective of the Ministry of National Languages and Social Integration is to consider each and every individual as vital link in the society, ensure the language rights of everyone and providing equal opportunities to every person."

These quotations, some of which I have highlighted in hold, are quite telling, reflecting the recognition of the importance of the individual, language and cultural diversity in the overall process of national integration and development in a post conflict Sri Lanka.

These more importantly reflect the involvement and total commitment of everyone to the success of the project.

6.0 Exploiting diversity for national integration and development

There are important lessons for Nigeria to learn from South Africa and Sri Lanka. Notice that there is emphasis on recognition accorded to the individual rights, language rights, and equal opportunities for every person as a vital link to the overall process of national integration and development. Recently, there have been calls for a national conference where Nigerians from all walks of life can sit together and talk about the different issues that affect Nigerians, including our diversity. The Federal government of Nigeria does not seem to be favourably disposed to this position. My personal opinion is that, a national conference is an absolute necessity in order to provide a platform for Nigerians to talk about their diversities, recognise that the well-being of every group and indeed of every individual is crucial to the overall well-being of the Nigerian nation.

If our national government is unwilling or perceived to fail to recognise individual and group rights, even with all the diverse colourings of our totality as Nigerians, it would be difficult to move towards national integration and development.

Having said that, there is a lot that individuals and groups can do on the path to national integration. Specifically, I shall restrict my discussion to what linguists can do to achieve a semblance of national integration and development.

As linguists, we can do a lot to achieve national integration and development. First of all, we are yet to address the number of languages in Nigeria. Yes, Ethnologue has 500 plus languages, but have we verified this number? Some of the information in

Ethnologue is dated; some are outright wrong. Therefore there is an urgent need for us as linguists to have concrete information through language surveys and mapping, on the actual, not purported, number of languages in Nigeria. One advantage of this is that every language will be captured and recognised, making the task of national integration easier. Secondly, it is imperative that we p have solid information on the level of vitality of our indigenous languages in Nigeria. Again, we can make reference to Ethnologue, but the same criticisms of inaccurate and dated information also apply. Today, the currency of language documentation is indisputable in Nigeria. When we document and describe languages, we are documenting and describing the culture of the people since language is an integral part of culture and it is the conveyor of culture. In other words, we are in effect projecting the culture of the people, sharing our knowledge of the people, their language with other groups, be they scholars, communities, individuals, etc. In so doing, we are directly and indirectly providing a platform for a better understanding of that language group. One way of doing this is to embed language documentation in outreach programmes, in addition to local documentation and description activities. A case in point is the Department of Linguistics & African Languages of the University of Ibadan, Recently, that Department was involved in language• documentation and description activities outside the South West geo-political zone where the University of Ibadan is located. I am I aware that they have been to Kwara State and towards the end of 2012 they were in AkwaIbom State working on the Iko language. I spent one year at the

Nasarawa State University, Keffi, in Nasarawa State. At the end of the year, I with the students familiarised ourselves with the phonology and morphology as well as the counting system of the Afo language, a highly endangered language spoken in Nasarawa and Plateau States - the only reference to it in published work is through a word list compiled by Armstrong in the 1960s (www.ethnologue.org). The 2011/2012 MA students of NSUK were working on writing up and possibly publishing a phonology of the Afo language. If each of us were to engage in more of such hands-on activity, there would be much more understanding of our indigenous languages and the rich cultural heritage that we are today ignoring to our peril.

For the more 'arm-chair' inclined among us, there is certainly more than one way to kill a cat. Linguists can be involved in the production of literacy materials including primers, dictionaries (online and print), reference grammars, from data obtained through language and cultural documentation. In spite of the large number of Nigerian languages (500 and counting!), there is certainly a paucity of reference grammars on our languages. A few of the reference grammars include those done by Wolff (1993) and Newman (2000) on Hausa and another one on the Oko language by Atoyebi (2010).

It seems to me that practicing linguists in Nigeria are fast becoming an endangered species! The number we turn out yearly and the number that is actually engaged in language related enterprise seems to be at great variance. I do not claim to know the number of linguists we turn out collectively from our universities annually. This is something we need to urgently compile. Given that we are talking about over 500 indigenous languages, I suspect that if we assisted communities in setting up language committees in their communities with a linguist as a consultant or collaborating partner, it would be easy to have basic documentation and description of the 500 languages within a five-year period. We do not necessarily have to work on our own languages; we could unearth fascinating materials in other Nigerian languages. When we have sufficient data on our local languages, the stage would have been set to prepare our languages for use in technological activities.

Speech technology, for instance, is an area that can be exploited for national integration and development. It is possible to produce synthesised systems that can be used to reach the millions of Nigerians who may not be literate in English or even in the local languages but can access information through modern technology tools wherever they are in their own languages.

Language data provides insight into the cultural practices of the speakers, including the knowledge systems. Some of us are sales agents to American and Chinese medicine and products through network or multilevel marketing. With documentation of various aspects of local knowledge systems, we would be armed with data that could proffer solutions to some of our seemingly intractable health challenges. We would then be in a position of being exporters of local knowledge in terms of traditional health care rather than mere consumers and importers. This has the potential of creating jobs, alleviating poverty; and ultimately culminating in national integration and development. This is just one aspect; the same can be replicated in the areas of education, agriculture, politics, etc. We would be on a path to self-discovery and national development.

Professor Chinyere Ohiri-Aniche, President of the Linguistic Association of Nigeria (LAN), has recommended that working on our indigenous languages can create jobs and alleviate poverty for the graduates we churn out every year if we engage them in the linguistic enterprise including, language surveys and mapping, language documentation and description, production of literacy and cultural materials, etc. This would provide excellent opportunities for our young and not so young linguists to work on languages other than their own, which will in turn lead to a better understanding of the people and culture of Nigeria, culminating in national integration and also developing the potentials of the citizenry. In addition, this will add to the self-worth of our graduates in contributing useful service to national development.

7.0   Outlook and conclusion

From the survey of the two countries, South Africa and Sri Lanka, language is a key index to national integration and national strategic planning. We have also drawn attention to the possibilities and potentials that abound when we have proper documentation and description of our languages. As linguists, we have bemoaned the absence of a well-articulated language policy in Nigeria. It is crucial for such a policy to be put in place in order to ensure that there is constitutional and budgetary provision for every Nigerian language which will ultimately provide a sense of belonging in the overall collective identity in our rich diversity.

The 'Working group' used to be a common feature of the West African Linguistic Society which was very productive leading to classic publications by Williamson, Dakubu-Kropp, etc. Now working groups have resurrected as research groups. I would like to propose a pragmatic venture that NAL may wish to undertake, which is to establish working groups along the lines of what used to obtain in WALS, to enable it investigate, compile, classify and publish the rich tapestry of various aspects of Nigerian languages and culture. A few groups that readily come to mind are the Phonology group, the Morphology group, the Syntax group, the Oral Literature group which will compile and analyse the various remarkable features of our languages. Of course, these are very broad groupings and we expect that there will be subgroupings. For instance, the oral literature working group is likely going to have a proverb and riddle work subgroup, a folktale group, a dirge group, a folksong group and other layers even within the subgroups. We will have something comparable to the World Atlas on Language Structures for Nigerian languages. It will be a phenomenal compendium of reference materials for all kinds of people interested in Nigeria's rich cultural tapestry.

On January 28, 2013, Luke Harding of the UK Guardian newspaper reported that fleeing Islamic insurgents in Mali set fire to a library containing thousands of priceless historic manuscripts which was tantamount to the destruction not just of the Malian/African heritage but of world heritage. Some of these were leather bound manuscripts dated from the 13th century detailing the unique record of sub-Sahara Africa's rich medieval history; such records debunked the claim that all of Africa had no written historical records but rather relied on oral tradition. Even though most of the documents were in Arabic, some were in African languages including Songhai, Tam ashek and Bambara on varied topics including astronomy, medicine, geography, religion, poetry music and women rights.

The danger is very real and threatening - many Nigerian children no longer have the opportunity to listen to folk wisdom from folktales, proverbs, riddles, traditional games and songs where local Nigerian languages are utilised. Rather they are glued to the television and computer screens, playing games and active on social media. Schaefer &Egbokhare (1999) have done a commendable job of documenting Emai narratives, which we are told is the "only published record of the oral tradition of the Emai people". Many of our over 500 languages do not have the luxury of having anything on record while the custodians, our elders, are exiting by the hour! Failure to engage in the documentation of our cultural and linguistic heritage can be likened to arson as reported in the case of the Mali Ahmad Babu Institute. It will amount to the razing of peoples' histories, knowledge systems, culture, religion and everything that make the people unique.

Although Nigeria seems to have an enormous number of languages, which is part of its rich tapestry linguistic and cultural heritage, his clear that many of these languages have a common lineage. The bulk of Nigerian languages (about 75%) are from the Niger Congo language family showing the relatedness of these languages as is reflected in the similarities in the basic vocabulary. Basically, there is therefore more that holds us together than the differences.

In this paper, we have only taken a peep into the Nigerian linguistic tapestry to whet our appetite on the various possibilities that we can unearth, were we to invest in the enterprise. The general theme of cultural tapestry evokes several cross cutting issues across the humanities, which I am certain would benefit from deeper exploration. I hope that the thoughts I have shared with us will generate more discussions on how we can truly integrate every language, every individual in the national development enterprise in order to utilise the ingrained capital from our rich cultural, tapestry.

Notes

* Aspects of this paper were presented at CLAN 2012, Adekunle Ajasin University, Akungba, Ondo State, December 3, 2012.
* FCT is the Fed ral Capital territory of Nigeria and not *strictu sensu* a state.

References

Achebe, Chinua 2)12. *There was a country: A personal history of Biafra.*
London: Penguin Books.

Awobuluyi, A 0. 1973. The modifying serial verb construction: a critique. *Studies in African Linguistics* 4/1:87-1 11.

Armstrong, Robert G. 1954. Talking drums in the Benue—Cross River region of Nigeria. *Phylon* 15/4: 355-363.

Atoyebi, Joseph Dde 2010. *A reference grammar of Oko*. Series editors: Wilhelm Moelig & Bernd Heine; Berlin: RuedigerKoeppeVerlag

Bamgbose, Ayo 1974. On serial verbs and verbal status. *Journal of West African Languages* 9/1:17-48.

1982. Issues in the analysis of serial verb construction. *Journal of West African Languages* 12/2:3-21.

1994. Pride and prejudice in multilingualism and development. Fardon, Richard & Graham Furniss (eds.) *African languages, development and the State*. London: Routledge.

Childs, G. Tucker 2003. *An introduction to African languages*. Amsterdam/Philadelphia: John Benjamins.

Crozier, David H. & Roger M. Blench (eds.) 1992. *An Index of Nigerian Languages* .2nd edition. Language Development Centre Abuja, Department of Linguistics & Nigerian Languages, Ilorin, Summer Institute of Linguistics Dallas.

Demuth, Katherine, Nicholas Faraclas & Lynell Marchese 1986. Niger Congo noun class and agreement systems in language acquisition and historical change. *Noun classes and categorization. Proceedings of a symposium on categorization and noun classification* Collette Craig (ed.). pp. 453-480. Amsterdam: John Benjamins.

Dimendaal, Gerrit J. 2001. Logophoric marking and represented speech in African languages as evidential hedging strategies. *Australian Journal of Linguistics*, Vol 21/1:131-157.

Dingemanse, Mark 2009. Ideophones in unexpected places.

Elugbe, Ben Ohi 1989. Edoid. The Niger Congo languages (J. Bendor- Samuel ed.). Lanham: The University Press of America. Pp 29 1-304.

Elugbe, BenOhi 1994. Minority language development in Nigeria: a situation report on Rivers and Bendel States. Fardon, Richard & Graham Furniss (eds.) *African languages, development and the State*. London: Routledge.

Elugbe, Ben Ohi 2011. *The scramble for Nigeria: a linguistic perspective*. An inaugural lecture delivered at the University of Ibadan 1992. Ibadan: DB Mirtoy Books.

Faraclas, Nicholas 1989. Cross River. The Niger Congo languages (J. Bendor-Samuel ed.). Lanham: The University Press of America. Pp 377-399.

Heiko, Narrog & Imelda Udoh. 2005. Elements of space grammar in Leggbo. *Journal of Asian &African Studies* No. 69:25-63.

Himmelmann, Nikolaus. 1998. Descriptive and documentary linguistics. *Language* 36: 161-195.

Hyman, Larry M. & Imelda Udoh 2007. Length harmony in Leggbo: a counter-Universal? *Linguistische Berichte Sonderheft* 14:73-92.

Ibli, Eugene U. 1998. Gender diglossia and mother tongue education in Ubang community of Obudu Local

Government Area. *Akamkpa Journal of Education* Vol.2:100-111.

Lawal, Adenike, S. 1989. The classification of Yoruba serial verb constructions. *Journal of West African Languages* XIXI2:3-14.

Nettle, Daniel 1996. Language diversity in West Africa: An ecological approach. *Journal of Anthropolgical Archaelogy* 15/4:403-438.

Nettle, Daniel 1998.Explaining global patterns of language diversity. *Journal of Anthropolgical Archaelogy* 17/4:354-374.

Newman, Paul. 1979. Explaining Hausa feminines. *Studies in African Linguistics* Vol. 10/2:

Newman, Paul 2000. *The Hausa language: an encyclopedic reference grammar*. New Haven: Yale University Press.

Pike, Kenneth L. 1948. Tone languages. Ann Arbor: University of Michigan Press.

Ron Schaefer & Francis Egbokhare 1999. (eds.) Oral tradition narratives of the Emai people. LIT Verlag.

Uwe Seibert's website on Language Ecology of Nigeria (accessed Sat June 22,2013).

Simmons, Donald C. 1956. Etotic Ibibio tone riddles. Man 56:79- 82.

Skutnabb-Kangas, Tove 2002. Language policies and education: the role of education in destroying or supporting the world's linguistic diversity. *Linguistic genocide in education: or worldwide diversity in human rights? Mahwah, New Jersey*: Lawrence Erlbaum. Pp296-374.

Skutnabb-Kangas, Tove2002.Why should linguistic diversity be maintained and supported in Europe?

Some arguments. Retrieved on July 25, 2013 from googlescholar.

Udoh, Imelda I. L. 2004. Ghost consonants and lenition in Leggbo. Journal of West African Languages XXXI.I:47-63.

------------------ 2007. Fortition and reduplication in Leggboideophones. *Journal of Languages & Linguistics* 28: 57-80.

Urua, Eno-Abasi2007. *'Abo die? language, life and sustainable development.* University of Uyo Inaugural lecture presented on August 27, 2007.

------------------ 2010. 'Come over to Macedonia and help us' - language documentation to the rescue! Paper presented at the workshop on Africa's response to language endangerment, University of Florida, Gainesville, December 2010.

------------------ 2012. Harnessing multilingualism and diversity for national integration and development. Lead paper presented at the Linguistic Association of Nigeria Conference at the Adekunle Ajasin University, Akungba, December 3,2012.

Ushie, Joseph A. 2011. Language as a fossil of history: Bette-Bendi and Bantu. Joseph A. Ushie & David L. Imbua (eds.) 2011. *Essays on the history, language and culture of Bendi.* Ibadan: Kraft Books Limited. Pp.139-166.

Ushie, Joseph A. Personnal communication - Friday August 2, 2013.

Veeramah, Krishna R., Bruce A. Connell, Naser Ansari Pour, Adam Powell, Christopher A. Plaster, David Zeitlyn, Nancy R. Mendell, Micahel E. Weale, Neil Bradman & Mark G. Thomas 2010. Little genetic differentiation as assessed by uniparental markers in the presence of substantial language variation in peoples of Cross River region of Nigeria. *BMC Evolutionary Biology* 10:92.

Webb, V. N. (2002). Language policy development in South Africa. Paper presented at the World Congress on Language Policies, Barcelona 16-20 APRIL 2002.

Welmers, Wm. E. 1973. African language structures. Berkeley: University of California Press.

Wolff, H. Ekkehard. *Referenzgrammatik des Hausa.* Münster: LIT, 1993. Coll.Hamburger Beiträgezur Afrikanistik ; no 2. Nigeria ranked 5th globally in language diversity – Brent Consulting (http://brenttconsulting.wordpress.com/2012/02/24/nigeria-5th-inlanguage-diversity/).

World Atlas on Language Structures www.wals.infohttp ://www.ethnologue.org Professor ChinyereOhiri-Aniche-personal communication October 2011

Acknowledgements

- NAL President and Executive Committee for inviting me to present this paper.
- Prof Ben Elugbe for sending me a copy of his published inaugural lecture.
- Prof Imelda Udoh for finding time to read through the draft paper.
- The University of Uyo for supporting my travel to the investiture.

The Artist as Griot: Two Knives in the Widow's House

Professor Chidi T. Maduka, FNAL

It is commendable that the organizers of this year's convocation chose this theme of The Literature of the ECO WAS Region, for it offers the members of the Academy the opportunity to closely examine the contribution of literature to the current struggle of the region s political leaders to ensure the political, economic and cultural unity of the various countries of the region. Although some scholars have previously focused their studies on the region, their treatment of the material dwells more on their perception of the authors (or texts) as belonging to the same geographical area arbitrarily put together by former colonial masters than sharing common political, economic and cultural affinities. We realize that this interpretation of the theme may be seen by some colleagues as unnecessarily tilting it towards the notion of literature as a phenomenon whose referentiality touches on various dimensions of social life rather than existing **sui generis** with its meaning being immanent in the text. However, it is reassuring that the issue which is multidimensional in character (and not just restricted to the two perspectives) has defied satisfactory resolution in most national literatures of the world. What is literature? What is criticism? These two questions, we believe, will probably provide as many stimulating responses as there are scholars interested in doing justice to the theme of the convocation.

Equally intriguing is the relative importance accorded the various literatures in European and West African languages such a Hausa, Igbo, Yoruba, Tiv, Izon, Ibibio, Kanuri, Akan, Ewe, Baule, Wolof etc. The practice of stressing the literatures in (what is regarded as) international languages (especially English and French) at the expense of those in the West African languages ought to be deemphasized. It is necessary for the various countries of the region to develop policies that would enable these languages and the literatures in them to play a role in the national development of each of the countries.[1]

But the interest of this paper focuses on another issue: the criticism of the literature. The current trends in the criticism of African/West African/Nigerian texts call for reflection. What makes it imperative for me is the accumulated experiences I have gathered as an observer of the various performances of oral literature in my community, and as a member of the panel of judges for the annual awards in literature organized by the Association of Nigerian Authors (ANA). The title of my paper is now taking shape.

First, the griot. Many scholars (e.g. Okpewho, Blair, Finnegan, Awoonor, Sekoni, Azuonye, Senghor) have reminded us that the artist in the oral tradition is basically a griot who is so multitalented that he can be at once a singer, a dancer, a poet, a novelist, a dramatist, a historian and even the living community library. This paper argues that contemporary writers in various languages (French, English, Hausa, Yoruba, Igbo, Tiv, Wolof, Akan, Ewe, Idoma, etc.) are all griots (or should be so). Second, the sub-title which is an Igbo proverb telling us that the widow is so poor that she lacks the means to have a well-functioning knife at home, hence the one that is sharp has no handle and the one that has a handle is not sharp. The theories being currently used in studying African/West African/Nigerian literatures are not only far removed from the African/West African/Nigerian cultural experience but also becoming so sophisticated that they disfigure rather than explain the significance of the texts. Abiola Irele feels so uncomfortable with them that he refuses to use them in his recent study dealing with the variegated strategies deployed by selected authors of African ancestry in coming to terms with the contemporary obfuscating European cultural presence in Africa and the Diaspora. In the introduction to the book, **The African Imagination: Literature in Africa and the Black Diaspora,** he tells the reader that the philosophy of literature used in the studies is informed by the ideas characteristic of the traditional approach to sociology of literature. On the other hand, the one that has a handle is very poorly developed as a viable option for studying African/West African/Nigerian literatures in foreign and indigenous languages. It is now opportune to give the trajectory of the varieties of positions taken by scholars within the two camps.

II

Africa/'West Africa is virtually a cultural satellite of the West in this era of globalization. The process indeed dates back to the Berlin Conference of 1884-1885 where European colonialists met (over drinks and pleasantries?) to carve out spheres of influence for themselves in Africa populated by the sub-human natives as they perceived the inhabitants. With time the subject peoples adjusted their mindsets to the thought processes dictated by the demands of the institutions of slavery, colonialism and neo-colonialism. The crucible of socialization reached its apex after the Second World War when the colonialists consolidated their imperialistic interests in world politics by deciding to form such international bodies as World Bank, Paris Club, International Monetary Fund (IMF) and World Trade Organization, and ensuring that they effectively control their operations. It is not surprising that Africa/West Africa finds it extremely difficult to wriggle out of the economic, political and cultural subjugation in which it has found itself, even though the situation would have been different if the rulers had patriotically flexed their muscles much harder.

The values that shape the people s lifestyle in Africa/West Africa do not basically derive their force from African cultural heritage, thereby turning the people into aliens in their various countries. In Nigeria, for example, it has become edifying to model the country s constitution on those from Britain and the United States of America, to proudly adopt English and French as the nation s lingua francas without thinking seriously about developing the indigenous languages and the literatures in them, to lionize foreign goods to the detriment of the locally made ones, to collude with multinational companies in looting the people s treasury and even to relish in investing the loots abroad and, to unwittingly denude the country of the top professionals who flee the nation for the rich, creative soils overseas where they eventually constitute a new breed of citizens fondly called the Nigerians in the Diaspora. The situation is even worse in the Francophone zone where many of the countries have proudly signed military pacts with their former colonial overlords and the Senghors elevated French language to the echelon of being the harbinger of African/West African civilization.

The emigration of many of the seasoned critics to Europe has quickened the pace of the Europeanization of the literary scholarship in the region. The general practice both in the classroom and personal research has been for the critics to use theoretical frameworks and concepts developed by European practitioners. Classicism (with Artistotle s **Poetics** as the anchor piece), Romanticism, Realism, Symbolism, Myth Criticism, Formalism, Marxism, Sociology of Literature, Psychoanalytical approaches, Structuralism are all used with abandon. Now contemporary approaches are religiously added to the list: thus all shades of Poststructuralism, Postmodernism, Postcolonial Aesthetics and Feminism are all cherished by the scholars. African texts are scrupulously subjected to analysis with the models and often African authors battered with criticism for not writing to the preconceived ideas.

Many African/West African scholars and Africanist scholars have produced works of enduring significance with the theories. However, the works are generally of limited importance to Africa because of their relative marginality to African cultural experience. For instance, Sunday Anozie has used the methodologies of the structuralist poetics in making erudite studies of the works of Soyinka, Okigbo, Tutuola and Senghor. His accomplishments forced him into a memorable encounter with Achebe whom he accused of stressing content at the expense of form in his works, making Achebe to call him a sterile imitator of European critical models.

Marxism has endeared its revolutionary aesthetics to many African/West African scholars. Biodun Jeyifo, for example, has fruitfully used it in many of his thought-provoking publications, especially **The Truthful Lie: Essays in a Sociology of African Drama.** Unfortunately, in this rigorously-argued book, he erroneously assumes that what he has developed as the three great **moments** in the development of the theory of literature in Europe (Aristotle, Hegel and Marx-Engels) applies equally to Africa, for Europe is merely a fragment of the universe. He concludes that Marx-Engel s moment stands for the ideal one valid for all humanity, since in it, protagonist and antagonist forces are not agents who carry an ineluctable tragic flaw which destroys them Rather , he continues,

> *they are individuals who carry the concrete goals and*
> *aspirations of social groups, forces or classes (1985:26).*

He then uses it to evaluate Soyinka s **Death and the King's** Horseman which he finds inferior to Hussein s **Kinjeketile**, a Kiswahili play in which the protagonist incarnates the spirit of the African resistance against German colonialism in East Africa, a representation that forcefully dramatizes the gallant historical exploits of the followers of the Maji Maji Movement. Such a parallel historical movement does not characterize the segment of Yoruba cultural history which provides the sub-soil of Soyinka s play. It would be hegemonic to impose a Marxist view of history on it: an alternative theory to account for its particularity needs to be developed. A look at Godwin Darah s The Political-Economic Factor in Urhobo Song-poetry and Tanure Ojaide s Poetry, Performance, and Art: **Udje** Dance Songs of Nigeria s Urhobo People points to the inadequacy of scholars privileging the methodology of moving from deduction (informed by, e.g., Marxist ideology) to induction (featuring the specific character of a people s culture) over the inductive-deductive paradigm which accords full space of being to the object of study. Darah s study which is predicated on Marxist methodology tends to restrict the free flow of Urhobo oral poetry by forcing it to revolve around its economic features as is usually the case with Marxist aesthetics, thus reducing the impact of its impressive erudite rendition. This may explain why African/West African/Nigerian historians generally prefer the use of the inductive-deductive methodology in studying the histories of local communities.

Other studies by Marxist scholars generally fall short of the ideal because of their dogmatic bent which overdetermines the role of economics in a people s social life, a phenomenon that a careful study of the African oral literature does not reveal. The limitation of the mode of criticism centres on its penchant for authoritarianism. The historic rebellion of some writers to it is recorded in The God **That Failed** edited by Richard Crossman.

Many African/Western critics incisively use the discoveries made in poststructuralism, a movement with many strands rooted in Saussure s postulations on the nature of the **signe** (sign), **significant** (signifier) and the **signifié** (signified). According to Saussure, a linguistic

115

sign is a complex whole made up of the signifier and the signified. The signifier is the word-image and the signified the concept evoked by the word-image. But the post-structuralists basically argue that truth or meaning is unstable since there is a perpetual cycle of the signifier undercutting meaning embedded in the signified, thus creating a world of multiplicity of meanings or even nihilism. Derrida celebrates this speech event in his deconstruction, Barthes in his **pleasure of the text**, Lacan in his **psychoanalysis**, Foucault in his **history and power**, Kristeva in y, her **intertextuality of texts**, Bakhtin in his **dialogism**, and Deleuze O and Quattari in their types of **délire** (desire).

All are rooted in relativism, a philosophical view of the world dating back to the sophist, Protagoras, noted for his aphorism that man is the measure of all things . In spite of its various strands in is philosophical thought, Robert C. Solomon s definition is of pertinent: EI1C

> *"Relativism ... seems to deny the obvious similarities among people and imply that we will never be able to understand one another - or find the truth - at all". (2009: 260). This view of the world is opposed to the African's/West African's who believes that truth can be discovered, however difficult it may be, and this for the sake of group interests. In spite of individual differences, the quest for locating the centre of meaning in the text beyond the caprices of possible solipsism is a worthy venture in African/WestAfrican criticism.*

Postcolonial aesthetics is not yet acceptable to some African/West African scholars probably because of its undue dependence on the wild conjectures of the reader (it is also rooted in Western relativism). Niyi Osundare, a vigorous opponent of the movement believes that the concept should be used to designate the period in succeeding the era of colonial rule in Africa.

Feminism stretches its roots to poststructuralism, especially the variant of Derridean Deconstruction which uses **aporia** - a form of irony - to undercut the essential character of propositions by revealing contradictions within them. It derives its radical posture of individualism to the movement S attachment to the philosophy dir of relativism. Women find it attractive because it enables them to discard the oppressive yoke of patriarchy which phallocentrically elevates male status in society as God-given (natural) and unassailable.

African/West African female critics feel alienated from the Western model of feminism which is rather arrogantly projected as being international in character. They reject some of its tenets as un African because they negate the principle of the complementanity of the Male and the Female in the creative order. This notable stance, however, has brought in its wake a medley of terms that call for proper articulation and possible harmonization: womanism, black womanism, fernalism, gynism, sitwanism, liberal feminism, radical feminism and motherism. Of great interest is Catherine Acholonu s **Motherism: The Afrocentric Alternative** to Feminism which boldly attempts to inject an African character into the theory, even though the execution does not match the grandeur of the vision (which derives its force from

African cultural heritage). The orientation seems to me much more attractive than the one in the book edited by Obioma Nnaemeka, one of the Nigerians living in the Diaspora. Entitled **The Politics of (M)Othering: Womanhood, Identity and Resistance in African Literature,** it contains many articles informed by the sophisticated, current European cultural and literary theories which are oblivious of African cultural view of life. African/West African critics are yet to produce satisfactory works imbued with the character of African/West African way of life.

Sociology of literature, the one practiced by Irele and most critics in the region generally captures the spirit of the African/West African mode of perceiving reality. It has, however, to probe more into the tenets of African oral tradition in order to domesticate it fully rather than depending solely on theories developed in Europe for its application in Africa/West Africa.

Of great historical importance is the recent influential **magnumopus, The Routledge Encyclopedia of African Literature** (2003) scrupulously edited by the erudite scholar Simon Gikandi and d appealingly packaged by the well-financed publishers Routledge. It clearly demonstrates the impotence of Africa with regard to the future development of her literature. Out of the 115 contributors, ing only 25 are resident in Africa. The well-researched comments as provided in places by Simon Gikandi on such movements as he Marxism, Structuralism, Poststructuralism and Postcolonial 1er aesthetics reveal the preponderant influence of European culture of on the development of African literature in this era of globalization. n: Although attention is given to the literatures in African languages ra1 they appear in the text more as museum pieces than vibrant aspects 115 of people s natural life.

The various departments of English and French in West Africa are the more or less cultural extensions of Europe in the region. The lecturers, the students and the curricula need to be decolonized to ian make sure that African/West African blood is satisfactorily injected [he into them. Literary scholarship should be made to derive its force of from the West African cultural experience. Bernth Lindfors s an observation is incisive:

> *Literary criticism remains the most underdeveloped of African arts. (2002. 6).*

The artists that the critics study are themselves generally well-informed about the oral tradition of their various peoples as can be seen from the literary and critical outputs of(e.g.) Soyinka, Achebe, Clark-Bekederemo, Rotimi, Okara, Amadi, Awoonor, Senghor, Dadié and Diop. It is necessary that the critics take steps to develop theories of literature rooted in the oral literatures of the various West African peoples. These theories will then be used fruitfully in studying all the literatures in European and West African languages. It is not sufficient for the critics to feel satisfied with making occasional forays into texts for the presence of the techniques of oral literature in them, as Kester Ogendi Echenim seems to be saying in the introduction to his book **Etudes critiques du roman africain francophone (Critical Studies of the Francophone African Novel**, 2010: x).

III

It is not necessary to rehearse the arguments that characterize the struggle for the de-Europeanization of the criticism of African literature some decades ago. (The struggle was more pronounced in the Anglophone sector of the African literary experience). The point to remember is that after the encounter between African scholars and the European critics who were establishing the canons for the criticism of the texts, the latter became more cautious and less impassioned in making oracular pronouncements on the texts. S The issue was so pervasive in the critical scene at the time that Dan Izevb aye, one of the pillars of the African literary criticism, had to base his doctoral thesis on. It, hence the topic The Relevance of Modern Literary Theory in English to Poetry and Fiction in English- speaking West Africa. It helped to shape his views which contributed a lot to the development of the literature of the Anglophone West Africa. Other Anglophone scholars whose works have made an impact on the literature of the region are Emmanuel Obiechina, Romanus Egudu and Robert Fraser. Obiechina, who is very strong in popular culture, uses his thought-provoking book **Culture Tradition and Society in the West African Novel** to basically stress the power of literacy on the development of the novel (among the members of the literate middle class) in West Africa. Egudu bases his work on the four West African poets: a: Okigbo, John Pepper Clark, Kofi Awoonor and Lenrie Peters and 'r rightly observes that they

> *...do not constitute a school in the conventional sense of the SI word, and there is neither the intention nor (sic) the attempt to present them as belonging to one. An accident of hi story if has merely located them together*

in the same geographical environment and cultural milieu, where historical forces have fostered for them similar intellectual growth and experiences in a very general sense (1986: ii).

and Robert Fraser takes the reader on a rewarding intellectual tour of West Africa while making his study of the poetry of the region.

He passionately yearns for a theoretical work on the

... an integrated African poetic which would enable us to make sense of written literature in European languages within a context determined by oral performances in the vernacular (1986: 7).

Many scholars anxiously wait for the realization of the dream.

The Francophone segment is alive with publications of theoretical significance, some of which use the primary texts by Anglophone authors (e.g. Achebe, Soyinka, Armah, Tutuola and Ekwensi) translated into French for the illustration of their points. Sunday of Anozie s text on the sociology of the West African novel written in French makes a rewarding reading. A section of it delineates a typology of the West African hero, fruitfully using the methodology the of Lucien Goldmann s Marxist-oriented genetic structuralism. Besides Thomas Melone s landmark performances in his three books on Negritude, Mongo Beti and Chinua Achebe, some is Nigerian critics in Francophone studies have also edified the critical scene of the region with their studies - Victor O. Aire with his work to on three Francophone novels and Echenim with his on the African Francophone novel in which he includes a comparative study of four heroes from the fiction of Kourouma, Achebe, Soyinka, Arrnah and Lundu.[2]

These selected critical works on West African Anglophone and Francophone literatures underscore the necessity of developing a strong theoretical base for examining the literary life of the region. it is equally incumbent on scholars to think seriously of incorporating the literary texts in the indigenous languages into their research interests because the region needs an integrated literary presence in Africa and the global village. It is therefore pertinent to discuss some critical works focusing on the study of the literatures in indigenous languages in West Africa because they illuminate the quest for an integrated body of knowledge embodying the collection of texts constituting the literature of the ECO WAS Region.

The works of Egudu, Olatunji, Ajuwon, Jega and Emenyonu come readily to mind. Romanus Egudu s **African Poetry of the Living Dead: Igbo Masquerade Poetry** is spectacular for its incisive grasp of the relationship between poetry, society and other art forms in Igbo traditional society. It is illuminating to learn that

> *Igbo masquerade poetry is essentially poetry of social control, social order and social harmony. It deals with the social, political, moral and economic aspects of life with a view to ensuring that people live well and peacefully as individuals and as a community (1992: 36).*

This is equally the findings of Olatunji and Ajuwon in their various studies of Yoruba oral poetry and Jega (with Bello-Kano and Saeed) on the Hausa one embodied in the public poetry of Mudi Sipikon.

Emenyonu s publications on the Igbo novel underscore the importance of Anglophone and Francophone scholars taking a great interest in the literatures in indigenous languages.

But the researches done by the writers themselves in this area of intellectual endeavour make the achievements of the scholars pale into insignificance. We have in mind Soyinka s original work on literary theory, Awoonor s provocative critical work, **The Breast of the Earth** (on which Obi Maduakor has done a very refreshing study), Dadié s publications on oral literature and Senghor s two volumes of essays on various topics on language, oral literature, African worldview and socio-political issues. All point to the necessity of West African literary scholars showing more interest in doing researches on oral literature so that they will be in a better position to develop valid alternative theories of literature rooted in African cultural experience and necessary for a better understanding of the texts in European and indigenous languages rather than slavishly using models developed in Europe.

Two major consequences may emerge from the scholar s reorientation of their research interests. The first will be their better appreciation of what the scholars in oral literature have been doing. For example, Isidore Okpewho, Chukwuma Azuonye, Helen asp Chukwuma,

F.B.O. Alcporobaro, Nkem Okoh and R. Finnegan, to mention but a few, ha ie constantly stressed the integrated nature of the African art form' (e.g. song, dance, poetry, drama, tale, graphic arts, music) which the griot dramatizes during the performance sessions of his art. This fact helps in the interpretation of African literature, especialiy that in European languages and even throws some light on the nature of poetry as understood in European literary tradition in which the issue of lyricism is often pushed to the limit of valorizing incomprehension as a virtue in creativity, whereas in the African tradition it is tied up to a context which elucidates its meaning.

The second is the recognition of the importance of Comparative the Literature in the curriculum. Through the discipline one clearly g a understands the interrelatedness of the various art forms and their affinities with other disciplines.

To fully conclude this section it is important to mention the topical book **Toward the Decolonization of African Literature** by Chinweizu, Jemie and Madubuike published over thirty years ago. The book is quite strong in its keen perception of the nuances of Eurocentrism in various aspects of African writing and scholarship, its insistence on the necessity of the critic having a clear, understanding of the African oral literature, its awareness of the pitfalls in the existing language and literature departments (1980: 296) and the suggestions for correcting them (298-299), and its call for the establishment of the department of Comparative Literature in order to enable the students to properly situate

African literatures vis-à-vis the other literatures of the world (298-299). Its major weakness lies in its use of the prescriptive if abusive **bolekaja** tone in disagreeing with critics and writers, thereby forgetting that there are as many logics of interpretation as there are critics, since literary experience is not at par with science. As for writers, they constitute a special breed of mortals who generally abhor being dictated to on how to write, as clearly revealed (e.g.) by Soyinka's M fury over their recommendations to him on how to become a good p poet, Achebe's rebuff of Anozie's attacks on him, Armah's pr onslaught on Larson for daring to dictate to the African novelist on in how to write, and Amadi's rejoinder to Omotoso for schooling him de on what form of vision of life/society should be best for his works. Their other shortcoming is their belief that the call for authors to U write works in the mother tongue is becoming anachronistic, hence hi their suggesting that the debate be suspended until the issue of the decolonization of African literature is settled.

All in all, the book does not provide a theoretical framework that serves as a sharp knife with a handle in the hands of the African critic. It has a handle but it is rather blunt like many other works.

IV

At this point it is necessary to sketch out a possible theoretical as position for interpreting West African texts in European and indigenous languages. Linda Tuhiwai Smith's classic **Decolonizing Methodologies: Research and Indigenous Peoples** calls for reflection. Although it is specifically written for the Maoris in New Zealand and Australia its observations apply equally to "indigenous an

Asian, American, Pacific and African forms of knowledge, systems of classification, technologies and codes of social life" (2012: 64). It ma is almost self-evident that when research is fully grounded in a people's culture, it tends to give a new sense of being to the people, of especially when the people have previously been viewed as an **object** without any sense of livingness and specific identity by an alien imperial and colonial power. From this perspective, as Smith rightly asserts, "the term 'research' is inextricably linked to European imperialism and colonialism" (2012: 1).

Two major strategies come readily to mind. The first tries to domesticate European methodologies in order to make them carry the weight of West African cultural experience. One can rationalize g the process by arguing that African forms of knowledge (e.g.

Mathematics, Philosophy and Physics embedded in Egyptian d pyramids and art forms from African traditional religion) have previously been borrowed by the enterprising European on intellectuals who used them to fertilize the healthy growth and development of European civilization from which emerge the theories in question. The approach informs the research of F.A.O. Ugiomoh, a young and dynamic scholar in African Art History. In his inaugural lecture entitled On **African Art and Identity Blogging: A Historical Perspective**, he tells us that the "theoretical tools I have relied on are drawn mainly from structuralism and post structuralism. And here particularly I mention hermeneutics at incorporating deconstruction" (2012: 18).

The second strategy, which the author prefers, builds on the discoveries rooted in the artistic performances of the griot in the people's oral tradition. From this perspective, the artist is perceived as a griot. In West Africa, as Dorothy Blair rightly tells us,

> *... the griots were the story-tellers, chroniclers, praise*
> *singers, poets, professional entertainers (1976: 25).*

Whether he/she is a poet, novelist or playwright, he/she is not only an artist but also a social critic who, through a clever manipulation of words, helps to put order in society by suggesting values that will make it better. The physical and biological sciences have a established the principle that order governs the complex operations of the universe. This order should implicitly prevail in society. Accordingly,

> *Literature ... deploys images from the physical, metaphysical, biological and social worlds such as stars, planets, heavenly bodies, winds, clouds, sky, water, tides, waves, lightning, thunder, earthquake, rains, snow, heaven, hell, spirits, gods, goddesses, God, satan, soil, plants, animals, human beings, aspects of social life and other disciplines to underscore the importance of order in the self; relationship with the other and the functioning of social institutions (Maduka,* **Taming the Beast***... 1976:20).*

The position can be clarified. Proverb, which figures prominently Ii in oral communication and equally serves

as an indispensable rhetorical tool in the oral-narrative performance of the griot, is a form of epigram, a sub-genre of poetry defined by Baldick as "a e short poem with a witty turn of thought; or a wittily condensed expression in prose" (Baldick 71). Helen Chukwuma rightly asserts that "... proverb is central to Igbo oral art. Further, the oral prose narrative is the queen bee of the oral literary corpus encompassing as it does other forms as proverbs, riddles, song all in a dramatic garb"(1994: 250).
.

One can therefore reasonably affirm that a literary work of art is an expanded proverb in which the author adroitly uses a medley of strategies to reveal his/her vision of life. And this vision articulates values necessary for helping individuals or society operate rationally by maximally exploiting the principle of order regulating the mechanics of existence. It is the absence of this order in Nigerian society embodied in the form of a beast that is responsible for corruption in Nigeria. To contain this corruption, it is necessary first of all to tame this beast by ruthlessly imposing a regime of order in the society.[4]

Two other concepts have to be examined: Prose poetry and the narrative (which can be in the form of drama or novel/short story). As the various art forms such as song, dance, narrative, poetry, drama, riddle, proverb,' visual arts generally operate as an integrated body of forms, THE SUB-GENRE OF PROSE POETRY should be exhumed to help interpret some aspects of the literatures written in European and indigenous languages (as well as the oral forms of the latter). A prose poem is defined as *a short composition employing the rhythmic cadences and other devices of free verse (such as poetic imagery and figures) but printed wholly or partly in the format of prose, i.e. with a right-hand margin instead of regular line-breaks (Baldick, 1990: 180).*

It is not popular in European literary tradition even though it was practiced by such established writers as Charles Baudelaire, Arthur Rimbaud, Oscar Wilde and T.S. Eliot. Since the African literary a experience is generally rooted in the oral tradition in which prose narratives fuse gracefully with poetry and vice-versa, it can effectively operate as a sub-genre. It could thus be defined as an art-form in which the poetic is encrusted on the narrative and the narrative encrusted on the poetic. If it is the former, it can appear graphologically like prose as in the long narrative prose poem, (Gabriel Okara's) **The Voice** or Keita Fodeba's **Aube Africain** an (**"African Dawn"**); if the latter, it can have the graphological of structure of a poem but reads like prose with well-crafted clusters of images embedded in it like Okara's "The Fisherman's Invocation" which has been rated poorly by many critics because of its strange g format, whereas it is a very successful prose poem coming from a in poet-griot like Okara versed in the Izon oral literary tradition. Tanure Ojaide's **The Tale of the Harmattan** and **The Beauty I Have Seen** read like tapestries of canvas pervaded with the complex rhythmic cadences of riddle, proverb and prose poetry crafted into them. Ojaide has a profound knowledge of the oral tradition of the Urhobo.

This methodology may be very useful in reading many texts that appear at first queer when viewed from the perspective of the European tradition of poetry/prose-fiction.

The second important issue to be examined is the place of plot in the narrative. Aristotle's insistence that plot should be the soul of tragedy has held its force for centuries in the development of the various European literary histories. It even contributed to some degree to the emergence of formalism as an important literary theory in the continent.

A careful examination of the narrative in the African oral tradition shows that character is central to the representation of the vision of life/society in the texts. This is probably because in the larger society individuals matter a lot in the evaluation of the orientation of moral codes of behaviour in society. It would therefore be useful to reconsider the narrative theories in drama and prose-fiction in order to give character delineation a privileged position in the totality of the techniques used in the representation of visions of life/society in the genres. Accordingly, all such other narrative elements as plot, setting, diction should be made to play subsidiary roles in the production of the total effect required of texts. (To Jonathan Culler, the great European structuralist scholar, character should constitute the energizing force of the narrative (1975: 12) but his fellow European theorists seem not to be interested in it).

An attempt should also be made to reorganize the programmes of the West African language departments in the universities. Thus, the students should be made to know how to read and write a West African language and be able to interpret the literature in it. A knowledge of oral literature should be made compulsory for both students and lecturers. And the discipline of Comparative Literature should be carefully cultivated in the appropriate departments so that literature will be properly understood as an integrated body of knowledge necessary for promoting unity among the various peoples of a country, region and the world. In addition, the concept of genres as handed down through colonialism should be re-examined in the context of the performances of the griot-artists in society.

Conclusion

To conclude briefly, West African scholars are urged to use the European critical theories with caution in studying the literatures of the region. This is because these theories are often formulated with ideas alien to the cultural experience of the region. It would be preferable for the scholars to closely study the discoveries so far made by scholars in the area of the region's oral tradition and to use them to formulate new theoretical constructs to be used for the interpretation of the texts in the region. Above all, the literatures in the indigenous languages should be made to assume their rightful place in the curriculum of the various departments engaged in the teaching of language and literature in the West African universities, and to do this successfully the discipline of Comparative Literature should be encouraged to take roots in the various universities.

Notes

1. See Chidi T Maduka's article "The Clouds Are Thickening: Nigerian Languages and Literatures in National Development" (2003).

2. The author has just seen a copy of African Literature: **A Anthology of Criticism and Theory (2009)** edited by Tejumola Olaniyan and Ato Quayson, whose contents seem pertinent to the issues under discussion. Unfortunately, he has not read it. It is published abroad, hence the difficulty of his having seen it in time.

3. See E.Nolue Emenanjo's "The Generic Determination of African Oral Literary Texts" (2000) for a detailed examination of the terms in critical usage in studying oral literature.

4. See Chidi T. Maduka's **Taming the Beast in the Body Politic: Culture, Nationhood and the Imperative of Order in Nigeria (2010).**

5. It is ideal to make the discipline to operate as a full-fledged department independent of other language departments but closely sharing bonds with them since they largely provide the subsoil of the values sustaining its life at a multinational level.

Works Cited

Acholonu, Catherine. **Motherism: The Afrocentric Alternative to Feminism.** Owerri: Afa Publications, 1995.

Ajuwon, Bade. **Funeral Dirges of Yoruba Hunters**. New York: NOK, 1982.

Anozie, Sunday. **Sociologic du roman africain.** Paris: Aubier, 1970.

Azuonye, Chukwuma. "Stability and Change in the Performance of Ohafia Igbo Singers of Tales", **Research in African Literatures**, No. 14, No. 3, 1983 (3 32-380).

Akporobaro, F.B.O. **Introduction to African Oral Literature.** Lagos: Princeton Publication Co., 1994.

Baldick, Chris. **The Concise Oxford Dictionary of Literary Terms**. Oxford: Oxford University Press, 1990.

Blair, Dorothy S. **African Literature in French**. Cambridge: Cambridge University Press, 1976.

Chinweizu, O. Jemie, I. Madubuike. **Toward the Decolonization of African Literature**. Enugu: Fourth Dimension Publishers, 1980.

Chukwuma, Helen. **Igbo Oral Literature: Theory and Tradition**. Abak: Belpot (Nig.) Co., 1994.

Crossman, Richard, ed. **The God that Failed.** New York: Bantam, n.d.

Culler, Jonathan. **Structuralist Poetics: Structuralism, Linguistics and The Study of Literature.** Ithaca, New York: Cornell Univ. Press, 1975.

Dadié, Bernard. **Légendes africaines** Paris: Seghers, 1954.

_____ **Un nègre a Paris**. Paris: PA, 1959.

Darah, Godwin. "The Political-Economic Factor in Urhobo Song- poetry". Ed. Georg Gugelberger. **Marxism and African Literature**. London: James Currey, 1985 (178-194).

Echenim, Kester Ogendi. **Etudes critiques du roman africain francophone**. Benin: Mindex Publishing, 2010.

Egudu, Romanus. **Four Modern West African Poets**. New York: NOK, 1977.

African Poetry of the Living Dead: Igbo Masquerade Poetry. Lewiston: Edwin Mellen Press, 1992.

Emenanjo, E.Nolue. "The Generic Determination of African Oral Literary Texts". Eds. Damian U. Opata and A.U. Ohaegbu. **Major Themes in African Literature.** Nsukka: AP Express, 2000 (35-53).

Emenyonu, Ernest. **The Rise of the Igbo Novel.** Ibadan: Oxford University Press, 1978.

Fraser, Robert. **West African Poetry: A Critical History**. Cambridge: Cambridge University Press, 1986.

Finnegan, R. **Oral Literature in Africa**. London: Oxford University Press, 1970.

Gikandi, Simon, ed. **The Routledge Encyclopedia of African Literature**. London: Routledge, 2003.

Irele, Abiola. **The African Imagination: Literature in Africa and the Black Diaspora**. New York: Oxford Univ. Press, 2001.

Jega, Attahiru M., Ibrahim Bello-Kano, Asma'u Garba Saced. **The Public Poet: A Biography of Mudi Sipikin.** Kano: Centre for Democratic Research and Training, 2003.

Jeyifo, Biodun. **The Truthful Lie: Essays in a Sociology of African Drama**. London: New Beacon Books, 1985.

Lindfors, Bernth. "Approaches to Folklore in African Literature" in ed. Bernth Lindfors, **Folklore in Nigerian Literature**. Ibadan: Caltop Publications, 2002.

Maduka, Chidi T. "The Clouds Are Thickening: Nigerian Languages and Literatures in National Development", **Journal of Nigerian English and Literature**, Vol.4,2003(11-19).

Taming the Beast in the Body Politic: Culture, Nationhood and the Imperative of Order in Nigeria. Public Lecture Series, School of Graduate Studies, University of Port Harcourt, Port Harcourt, 2010.

Maduakor, Obi. "Kofi Awoonor as Critic", **African Literature Today**, 19, 1994(8-20).

Meloné, Thomas. **Mongo Beti,l'homme etle destin**. Paris: PA, 1971.

Chinua Achebe et la tragedie del'histoire, Paris: PA, 1971.

De la negritude dans la littérature négro-africaine. Paris: PA.

Nnaemeka, Obioma ed. **The Politics of (M) Othering**. London: Routledge, 1997.

Obiechina, Emmanuel. **Culture, Tradition and Society in the West African Novel**. Cambridge: Cambridge University Press, 1986.

Ojaide, Tanure. "Poetry, Performance, and Art: **Udje** Dance Songs of Nigeria's Urhobo People". **Research in African Literatures**, 2001 (44-75).

Okoh, Nkem. **Preface to Oral Literature**. Onitsha: Africana, 2008.

Okpewho, Isidore. **The Epic in Africa Towards a Poetics of the Oral Performance**. New York: Columbia University Press, 1979.

_____ed. **The Oral Performance in Africa**. Ibadan: Spectrum, 1990.

Olaniyan, Tejumola & A. Quason, eds. **African Literature: An Anthology of Criticism and Theory**. Maiden, MA: Blackwell Publ, 2009.

Olatunji, Olatunde O. **Features of Yoruba Oral Poetry**. Ibadan: University Press, 1984.

Senghor, Leopold. **Liberté 1: Humanisme et négritude**. Paris: Seuil, 1964.

Liberté 11: Nations et voles africaines du socialisme. Paris:. Seuil, 1971.

Smith, Linda Tuhiwai. **Decolonizing Methodologies: Research and Indigenous Peoples**. London & New York: Zed Books, 2012, (2nd Edition).

Solomon, Robert C. "Hermeneutics and Pragmatism: Relativism Reconsidered" in Solomon Roberts. **Introducing Philosophy**. New York/Oxford: Oxford University Press, 2009(260-266).

Soyinka, Wole. **Myth, Literature and the African World**. Cambridge: Cambridge University Press, 1976.

Ugiomoh, F.A.O. **On African Art and Identity Blogging: A Historical Perspective**. Inaugural Lecture. Port Harcourt: University of Port Harcourt Press, 2012.